VICTORIAN CRITICAL INTERVENTIONS
Donald E. Hall, Series Editor

I0892186

The Old Story, with a Difference

Pickwick's Vision

Julian Wolfreys

The Ohio State University Press
Columbus

Library of Congress Cataloging-in-Publication Data

Wolfreys, Julian, 1958–
The old story, with a difference : *Pickwick*'s vision / Julian Wolfreys.
p. cm.—(Victorian critical interventions)
Includes bibliographical references and index.
ISBN 0–8142–1021–X (alk. paper)—ISBN 0–8142–5149–8 (pbk. : alk. paper)—ISBN 0–8142–9098–1 (CD-ROM)
1. Dickens, Charles, 1812–1870. Pickwick papers. I. Title. II. Series.
PR4569.W65 2006
823'.8—dc22
2005033690

Cover design by Dan O'Dair.
Type set in Adobe Garamond.
Printed by Thomson-Shore, Inc.

The paper used in this publication meets the minimum requirements of the American National Standard for Information Sciences—Permanence of Paper for Printed Library Materials. ANSI Z39.48–1992.

9 8 7 6 5 4 3 2 1

For J. Hillis Miller

Oui, il y a de l'amitié à penser

Contents

Acknowledgments and a Note on the Text

This book first appeared to me in a somewhat disguised, not to say truncated form during the summer of 2004, in a course at the University of Florida on Victorian Literature. I would like to thank the students who participated in that course for their insights on *Pickwick* in particular and Dickens in general. I would like also to thank Donald E. Hall and Heather Lee Miller for their enthusiasm for and encouragement of this project. In addition, both Jim Kincaid and Dan Cottom provided a number of crucial critical interventions in response to a first draft of the book while still in very rough manuscript form; I would like to thank furthermore the anonymous member of The Ohio State University Press's editorial board for additional comments on the manuscript, which allowed for timely revisions of some important points. The most invaluable contributions to and enthusiasm for this project have, however, been Xu's, without which this book would not have assumed quite the shape it has.

All references to *The Pickwick Papers* are taken from Mark Wormald's edition of the novel (London: Penguin, 2003) and are cited parenthetically as *PP.*

Introduction

> Centuries are the children of one mighty family, but there is no family-likeness between them. We ourselves are standing on the threshold of a new era, and we are already hastening to make as wide a space, mark as vast a difference as possible, between our own age and its predecessor.
> —Letitia Elizabeth Landon, *On the Ancient and Modern Influence of Poetry* (1832)

> Fundamentally, form is unlikeness . . . every difference is form.
> —George Eliot, "Notes on Form in Art" (1868)

> So much we can see; darkly, as through the foliage of some wavering thicket . . .
> —Thomas Carlyle, *Sartor Resartus* (1833–34)

I. *About* This Book

In addressing at length Charles Dickens' first novel, *The Posthumous Papers of the Pickwick Club* (1836–37), what is this book *about?* What does it think it is doing, and around what focal points will it circle? The visible, visuality, visibility, vision, visions, visualization, invisibility, view, prospect, observation, perception, sight, insight, hindsight, foresight, introspection, retrospection, eyes, reflection, appearance, spectacle, spectacles, optics, magnification, apparitions, phantasms, microscopes, telescopes, focal point, dream, looking, gazing, glancing, mental picture, hallucination.

Not every term here will be treated in equal measure. However, each in some manner will be seen to touch upon every other, and so to inform the skein of words, the lines, motions, and rhythms they enable, and the images they shape, giving us to apprehend and to imagine that which we cannot see with the naked eye, from page to page across the novel. We are dealing here with the intimate proximity *and* unbridgeable distance by which sight touches. Each term is of significance to the ways in which *The Pickwick Papers* makes us feel and, equally importantly, perhaps "before all," makes us *see* (Conrad 1988, xlix). The echo of Joseph Conrad's famous statement concerning the work of narrative art is deliberate, for it announces a relationship between differing senses of sight with regard to what the literary can or at least strives to cause to appear, and the effect that such an appearance can produce. That which is caused to appear, or which by chance we might come to see, can involve reception of, and reflection on, the work of memory, or traces of the past. Where this is the case, such manifestations will be addressed through consideration of envisioning.

Having stated my focus as starkly as possible, I would like to make a few brief comments on what *The Old Story, with a Difference:* Pickwick*'s Vision* is *not about.* It is not about text and context, at least not in any direct or straightforward fashion. Nor is it about *Pickwick*'s relation to "history" in any simple manner. My concerns are not to do with understanding the history of the period, even though, inevitably, some of the novel's relation to the historical and the issues in which they are intertwined will arise. I am not claiming to present through my reading a view of history, nor should my reading of the text be considered in terms of either a return to history or a consideration of what John Brannigan has described as "the status of history" in the text (1998, 2). I will have occasion to trace or otherwise allude to certain histories, or particular genealogies and "archiviologies," to borrow Jacques Derrida's neologism (1996a, 34).[1]

Inevitably it will be necessary to make clear particular material and cultural and historical resonances as these solicit the structure of *Pickwick.* But it has to be said from the outset that no sustained effort is made in the present volume either to historicize or to contextualize *Pickwick,* if by either "historicization" or "contextualization" one understands a process of grounding the literary text, and thereby stabilizing meaning or identity. Such processes venture making the strangeness of literature safe, of domesticating, corralling, and policing its play. They can often be read as aiming to construct for the text if not one stable meaning then a structure of meanings commensurate with one another, through the tracing of aspects, assumptions, or ideologies of a text as if these were simply the signs of its historical moment and that this were all that made up the literary text.

Critical gestures and practices of historical contextualization run the risk of reducing both the literary text and the act of reading to instrumentality. And if this is true of straightforward acts of historicization, arguably it is even more the case in modes of reading where the text's only use-value is as an exploitable phenomenon for exposing and exploring the power relations of a particular social, cultural, ideological, and historical moment. Such a reading might claim that *Pickwick* enacts through its modes of comedic representation a series of momentary subversions of cultural manifestations of power via parody, pastiche, satire, or whatever, only to witness the closure of subversion and a return to order in a vision of sentimental benevolence.

However, what is overlooked in such a manner of reading is the literary text as *literary;* any "mode of analysis . . . that sees the text as an organicist unity or uses it for a totalizing purpose (as when the right or the left speaks for history) is *blind*" to the literary (Hartman 1989, 19; emphasis added). What goes unseen are those instances of dissonance that exceed dissidence, which allow the reader a reflection *on* and *of* his or her being and agency as being marked by difference. To read in this fashion and to insist on the significance of the literary text is not to suggest literature or the literary as privileged mediums, or of being more significant than other forms of document. It is, however, to insist on the singularity of the literary, the grammar, rhetoric, and on the discursive networks that mark it as what it is and not something else. The literary, in its modes of envisioning and representation, might allow us to see the other of history. For in the literary—this uncanny phenomenon that cannot be given the identity of *concept,* but which is more precisely a barely discernible notion—"the true *image* of the past flits by. The past can be seized on as an *image* that flashes up at the moment of its recognizability" (Benjamin 2003, 390). Whatever the literary might be, however we might define provisionally the probably undecidable structures and manifestations of this disquieting, hybrid, quasi-identity, it comes to articulate the past, but not by recognizing it as it was. Instead, it may be said, after Walter Benjamin, that the literary appropriates "a memory as it flashes up in [that] moment of danger . . . [that] threatens both the content of the tradition and those who inherit it" (391).

The "literary" is thus irreducible to and incommensurable with discourses of history, sociology, or politics. If *Pickwick* is a success in the early nineteenth century, this is because it signals to its readers through those parodic imaginary visions of a recent past a constellation of cultural identities available to memory, and which are in danger of being forgotten in the desire to mark as great a distance from that past as rapidly as possible. In this *Pickwick* announces the crisis—that which Benjamin identifies as danger—of the moment as a crisis of vision and representation, even as it affords its readers a glimpse of the difference of their being from their predecessors and their becoming different. How does one see oneself in seeing one's difference from one's parents? And how may this vision maintain the traces of the past without being overwritten by them? What are the proper perspectives for the reiteration of particular visions of Englishness?

This is in part what *Pickwick* may be seen—and read—as bringing into the light, through a double process of focalization that simultaneously looks to the past and to that which is to come. In this way, the reader is "enabled to find and recognize himself in the actions of the fictitious individual" (Costa Lima 1988, 135) but also to perceive one's difference in the imaginary vision of the fictional individual's failure to see oneself in the proper light, and thus to be a *figure* of fun, the prosopopoeic manifestation of a tropological cultural structure. The structure of vision is one that therefore offers the chance of producing for the reader what J. Hillis Miller calls a *self-reading* (of which I shall have more to say, below; see Miller 1987, 81). However, in order to apprehend this structure the literary text must be read on its own terms, and this is what I seek to do here, examining a range of tropes, metaphors, motifs, and other figural and structural devices to do with vision and all its non-synonymous cognates.

Also, in reading *Pickwick* I am not making claims about the novel in general or as one manifestation of "literature" or "the literary." No statement about the literary text can be raised justifiably to a concept, much less a generalization. For this reason "literature" can "only be exemplified and the examples will of course all differ" (Miller 1991, 231). We cannot, and must not, program our reading of the literary, whether according to a generalizable politics of reading, or in instituting a program, a method of reading, repeatable from text to text. The application of and, more importantly, *to* historical context is simply one means by which we generalize, stabilize, and resort to the program or method of analysis. What is missed—what remains here and here but unseen—in such acts of reading is, as I have just stated, that every example on which we draw will necessarily differ from every other.

Therefore one must come to see the text as other, and as a singular other. Ethically, the demand of reading is to respect and respond to the singularity of the text, as far as possible. This strange entity we call the literary is a unique weaving because, unlike any other mode of production, it produces virtual, visual realities generated by the oddity of a specific form of interrogation. This demand is encapsulated in the demand: *what if?*—which subsequently we respond to by proposing an answer through the fiction of the *as if.* (Of this figure—*as if*—there will be more to say, particularly in the afterword.) Answering such a question produces phantasmic, imagined worlds that, when you come to think of it, are not a little uncanny *because* they are so like the realities we inhabit *and yet* they are not wholly like them, either. Thus literature and the literary offer us innumerable countersignatures to the real, to "history," to the past. If "the past is a foreign country" then the literary is its language (Hartley 2004, 1).

Or let us say it is apprehensible, at the very least, as a translation and memory machine. The literary is, we might say, a mnemotechnic communicating, albeit partially, improperly, and in a ruinous fashion, between heterogeneous historical or material instances. The literary can remind us, if we are open to its call, that its acts of envisioning are inescapably and intimately implicated in the becoming of our identities. The literary is that name for a certain exteriorization of memory and its phantasmagoria, which figure a significant aspect of our being, and by which we are haunted. With this in mind, therefore, I seek to explicate in the present volume not so much a direct understanding of the historical and its traces as a reading of the translation of particular motifs and signs already adverted, as these in turn are implicated in the projection of certain cultural identities and the processes of their becoming. Furthermore, I do so with an eye toward how these mediate and are mediated by the workings of memory and a sense of the past. Or instead say *pasts*—for there is more than one past at work in *Pickwick* that comes momentarily into view. In addition to the matter of "history," these have to do with memory, intertextuality, and being. There are others, doubtless. But it is only on the fewest examples that we will focus.

II. *About* the Title (Oblique Illumination)

So much for what this book is about; but what of our title—*The Old Story, with a Difference:* Pickwick's *Vision*? Deliberately cryptic, it nevertheless provides the reader with an oblique illumination or illustration—illumination of that illustration and illustration of how illumination takes place—of the work of those figures and tropes that were announced at the very beginning of this introduction. There is much that circles about the structural and semantic relations of the title that is not merely playful. In a performative manner, and in the spirit of that mockingly obtuse first sentence of *The Pickwick Papers* (itself concerned with illustration and illumination, as we shall have occasion to observe), our title brings before the reader's eyes all the concerns of this study, even though they may as yet remain invisible. This being the case we would therefore beg our readers' indulgence for the following circumlocution.

About this title, at which the good reader will have *looked* carefully: *The Old Story, with a Difference:* Pickwick*'s Vision.* The question is one of what will have been seen there or otherwise overlooked. (And this is very much apropos *reading* and *seeing Pickwick* critically.) After all, titles, like citations, "give the tone through the resonance of a few words, the meaning or form of which ought to set the stage" (Derrida 1996a, 7). *Ought to* indeed, though this conditional caveat announces the impossibility of guaranteeing the attention given to looking—which is also to say reading—and the manner of perception.

If the anastomosic link I seek to bring into view between *looking* on the one hand and *reading* on the other seems, if not swift, then at least fanciful, it should be remembered that *perception* is that act of sensuous or mental apprehension, whereby knowledge has the chance both of being collected and received. *Perception* appears to announce that which makes the connection between seeing and reading, and which might be missed in the seemingly merely technical term *looking. Perception* announces that "indispensable sense of imaginary . . . vision [that] tends to involve both actual looking and interpreting, includ[ed] in literary reading" (Bal 2002, 37). What might have been seen *or* overlooked, received or missed, in a title is all the more crucial when that title, or part of it at least, *is also* a citation, however *invisibly* this might pass us by, and especially when it is a case of "capitalizing on an ellipsis" (Derrida 1996a, 7). Such capitalization, and the ellipsis that makes it possible, is observable only *if one perceives the citation* paradoxically by its absence. A concern is announced with what escapes and exceeds empirical observation in the chance of other modes of vision, perception included. Yet whether or not one notices the absence of that mark announcing an erasure, the force of its opening is still in operation, and perhaps all the more forcefully so for being invisible to the naked eye. Perception of the citation as citation might bring back that which has been excised or repressed in the inscription, that which is not seen coming back partially to the mind's eye as it were, as the sign that sight or vision of particular kinds are inextricably bound up with memory, and with a certain acuity with regard to in*sight* apropos the past.

This is what my title announces, however elliptically. In effect what is inscribed in the title is also what the title gives us to see. There are thus two focal centers in the title. Or let us say, more precisely, in the *two parts* of the title, one on each side of the colon, observation of which encourages a binocular rather than a monocular examination. On the one hand, there is the matter of seeing, of vision, of sight and interpretation. My title comments on the translation effects of sight and vision, as these are observed to take place in *The Posthumous Papers of the Pickwick Club.* One particular aspect of the translation is its rendering of the past. This takes place throughout *The Pickwick Papers* through the generation of the images and phantasms belonging to a phenomenal reality produced by sight, by looking, by the response to visions and other phenomenal manifestations. On the other hand, there is that interest in narrative transmissibility, and the concern with the ways in which marks, signs, and traces of the past (*the old story*) come to be transmitted through their iterability (*with a difference*), in order that the reader might have the chance to *see* the past, though never as such, only through the interpretive lens by which the materiality of history is transformed into the materiality of the letter (on which materialities and their significance to this study, along with a third, the materiality of vision, I shall comment further in the introduction).[2]

Hence the matter set out in plain sight before the reader, even though everything that is *there,* in the title, is not necessarily revealed instantaneously or to the same degree for every reader. Seeing and reading take time; duration cannot be anticipated; revelation is uncertain, its effects uncontrollable and unreliable; and perception, that sensuous apprehension or sentiment in response to the visions, images, and apparitions of introspection and retrospection, is not always trustworthy as it attempts to traverse the gap between one historical moment and another, in an act of imaginary "focalization." I take the term "focalization" from the work of Mieke Bal. As Bal points out, "focalization" is equivalent neither to "look" nor "gaze" and yet touches on both concepts. Instead, it names "what becomes visible through the *movement* of the look" (Bal 2002, 37, 39). Perceiving such acts of apparition and manifestation projected, illuminated, and engendered in such movement is intrinsic to my reading of *Pickwick.*

Thus what is staged in the title does not concern the title only, as already implied. Were that the case, everything I have said thus far would seem hyperbolic, unnecessary, gratuitous. Misperception, that is to say distorted vision and misreading, might lead particular readers to take that which is taking place as, say, poststructuralist cliché,[3] supposing such a thing—poststructuralism—to exist. In giving the tone, that which is at stake in the title also announces, however elliptically, the interests both of this reading of Dickens' first novel and that which is already mapped by

Dickens himself. I proceed through the reading of vision and its related tropes in the novel in order to respond to and thus *review* Dickens' apprehension of how one sees, and interprets, albeit obliquely, one's own historical moment and, through that, one's past as one seeks to envision a cultural identity marked by difference from, and yet intimately indebted to, processes of historical becoming.

So much for what my title is *about:* what it circles around, what *I* am circling around in discussing its implications and relations to the reading of *Pickwick,* as well as what—to recall the various resonances that inform *about*—it seeks to get under way, what it sets in motion, what it intends, to draw on the various meanings that play *about* its surface. Now, to that surface, in conclusion of the first part of the introduction; to its double or binocular structure by which is intimated the desire to have the reader look about them in different directions, almost simultaneously.

The first part of my title is that partial citation to which I have already alluded, taken from *The Posthumous Papers.* It comes from chapter 46, and a conversation between Samuel Pickwick and his lawyer, Mr Perker: "'it's the old story I suppose?' 'With a difference, my dear Sir; with a difference,' rejoined Perker, deliberately folding up the paper and putting it in his pocket again" (*PP* 624). A scene of narration and iterability then, as the words between the two men attest, and which iteration is staged in its spacing and temporal relay a little further on in the conversation, as a single phrase—"to remain here!" "To remain here?" "To remain here, my dear Sir"—oscillates between the two men (624). The two remarks, conjoined and edited unreasonably in my title, serve somewhat economically to announce Dickens' understanding of historical transitions in narrative and cultural transmission and translation, especially as those transformations, those differences, when brought before the gaze of the reader announce the historicity of difference, whereby an unsuturable gap between the old story and its difference *remains.* And to push the strong reading, what remains, the visible signs or remnants of "the old story," is only ever available because it is relayed *with a difference,* and thus has its chance of coming to be perceived or apprehended at differing historical and cultural moments—*here* and *here* and *here.* Therefore, within any given moment in which we read, the past informing that moment may be glimpsed, however obscurely—this is what comes *to remain here* but never simply as itself. One is thereby afforded the chance of a view of how the present moment both comes into being and how it strives to mark its difference from its predecessor, to echo the words of Letitia Elizabeth Landon above (1999, 1206).

However, this is not only a matter of the mark, sign, or trace. This moment between the lawyer and his client is a scene also of eyes, looks, gazes: Mr Perker is observed in passing "glancing eagerly at Mr Pickwick out of the corners of his eyes" (624). That view askance affords the reader a moment typical of *Pickwick*'s structures of vision and perception, as we shall have occasion to observe in the following chapters; hence my choice of this narrative scene as being exemplary of the work of the narrative as a whole. For what is to be seen here, looking slightly to one side or back at the implied position of the reader, is that he or she is invited simultaneously to observe the scene, witnessing Mr Pickwick and his responses to his lawyer, and also to watch Mr Perker looking at Mr Pickwick. The structure of looking is one of difference and relay, and possibly what might be termed anamorphosis or refraction (discussed further in the first chapter). I use the last term somewhat loosely. It may be said, though, and with some justification, that in being directed to look at *how* Perker gazes, the reader's eye becomes redirected in such a manner as to be able to observe both Pickwick and Perker and to register the *type* of look; or, to put this another way, to take note of the rhetoric of the gaze on this occasion. That this is made possible can be seen through the agency of the narrative eye, which sheds a light on—thereby changing the direction of narrative illumination—a specific location in the representation as a whole. Within the apparently simple scene a structural displacement occurs. Illustration provides illumination not only of itself but also of *how* illustration illustrates and illuminates, the temporal difference by which reading and seeing the phenomenal reality thereby being made visible. This difference-within-vision echoes that relay named iterability that we have already had occasion to view in the verbal exchange.

Briefly in conclusion of this section of the introduction to the second part of my title: Pickwick*'s Vision*. Much about this may be said to have come into focus already. I wish to pause over its structure a little more, however, before proceeding. Note that the possessive in the phrase is a double genitive. It articulates the structure of the expression even as it displaces from within univocal meaning and, with that, any single perspective. Both objective and subjective, it announces and identifies both the vision of the world of *Pickwick,* the novel and the trope of vision with which so much of the novel is interested in offering as examples of vision at work. The world of *Pickwick,* then: how one comes to see that world, how its characters see, or believe they see—themselves, their friends, and those all around them—and how seeing is always prone to distortions in its involvement with narrative apprehension.

III. Vision's Difference

Another double genitive: the difference by which vision is enabled, or by which a vision comes to appear, and the difference to any thinking of the past that the idea of vision makes. *The Old Story, with a Difference:* Pickwick*'s Vision* opens to the reader particular views of *The Posthumous Papers of the Pickwick Club,* to the visions and sights it stages. The perspectives and views offered here are of course those that the novel already anticipates *with a difference,* and to which my reading is therefore merely a response. What comes to be seen is that *Pickwick,* a rhizomic excess not easily containable by critical commentary, intervenes in, ruptures, and remakes the narrative mediation of a tripartite and heterogeneous identity through the projection of successive vignettes and stereotypes.[4] The facets of the identity and the modes of its becoming thus envisioned involve the English middle classes, a particular sense or manifestation of Englishness and, with that, the identity we now refer to with hindsight as "Victorian." How it achieves this, and how the novel may be read as communicating its singularity with regard to the vision it produces, is what is to be explored. As if it were some strange kaleidoscopic optical device, *Pickwick* may be said to illuminate through sharp and often satirical juxtaposition a few of the ways in which those heterogeneous middle classes we call the Victorians saw themselves, and how they believed they saw themselves becoming different in distinction from previous generations through their experience of events and occasions still haunted by the traces and structures of earlier cultural practices and beliefs.

In order to pursue this explication, my reading engages with those narrative codes of the novel already anticipated in my title, and illustrated above. Particularly, what is of concern throughout *The Old Story, with a Difference* is what I take to be an early nineteenth-century concern, perhaps even an obsession: how does one *view* the past? How does one *perceive* the relationship between the after-time of narrative and the materiality of history, the traces of which become rematerialized through the phantasmic view afforded by the narrative? What might be the roles of memory or feeling, phenomenological perception and introspection in the translation between the events or facts of the past and verbal or visual anamnesis in its manifestation as storytelling? The emphasis on the visual throughout my introduction is not chosen carelessly, as should now be plain. As I have argued already and will continue to show in detail, such figures are central to *Pickwick*'s modes of production. Take, for example, two figures having to do with visualization and graphic iterability, stereotyping and the vignette, both of which in this double relation announce those concerns that mobilize my title. Moving our understanding of these terms beyond the purely technical, it will be argued that the novel's embedded tales (which will be considered in my final chapter) are vignettes in a very particular, if idiomatic manner. Serving as "illustrations," via which the connection between narrative and visualization becomes foregrounded, as with the more conventionally understood vignette, the tales appear for the most part at the ends of chapters. Dickens' use of the tales partakes of both senses of vignette, the printed ornamental design and the photograph. In doing so, it causes through narration and the personal memory of the past on which that narration relies the momentary visualization of that past. Such an act of envisioning is double, because the narrative produces its image both intra- and extradiegetically—for the characters in *Pickwick* to whom the tale is being told, and to the readers of *Pickwick.* Through processes of cultural stereotyping Dickens causes us to "see" the anachronistic being of particular characters, including Samuel Pickwick, and thus to see ourselves in our perception of our differences from them. The stereotype and vignette may serve as the vehicles for satire and parody, and with that the caricatured delineation of particular facets of Englishness, but in these modes, sentiment and affection as the articulations of memory—and the images so encouraged—are also at work. What occurs perhaps is the possibility that the reader might come to envision the other within oneself, or otherwise to see oneself in the mind's eye as the same, though with a difference.

It should be remarked, however, that, in considering the projection of English cultural identities in the early part of the nineteenth century it is not that *Pickwick* shows its readers to themselves directly. The novel is not a mirror or simple representation of its times; at least, it is neither solely nor simply that. Rather, if the reader comes to *see* oneself, partially or at all, it is as through a glass darkly, to echo Carlyle's own distortion of *Corinthians* (1991, 84).[5] Carlyle's ruined citation, taken as one of the epigraphs to this chapter, itself belongs to an attempt to address the problem of reading, narrating, and deciphering the past and the present moment of inscribed reflection in relation to whatever is taken to be the past, as this comes to be apprehended through the motif of vision. And it is important to understand that the double question of perception and perspective, whether one sees empirically or in the mind's eye, is bound up closely with the comic structures of *The Pickwick Papers.* Distortion of vision—performatively doubled in Carlyle's "pastoral" reinvention—gives access to comic perspectives, which, by their modality, acknowledge (as I have observed) the difference between, and therefore the visible forms of, one age and another. This in turn makes and marks as wide a space, as vast a difference as possible, to paraphrase the words of Letitia Elizabeth Landon. What comic, often satiric comparative critique brings into focus is that every difference, on which the comic effect of initial resemblance relies, in differing formally produces its own image through unlikeness rather than similarity, to invoke George Eliot's aphoristic apprehension, given above (1990, 232).

IV. The Representation and Rhetoric of Becoming

Already implicit in what has been said so far is the fact that however one speaks of a historical moment what is at stake always involves a double question: of narration and representation, and the continuous movement therein between the verbal and the visual. One writes, delineates an event, a series of events, a period of time, and one does so in response to the reception of so much white noise, so many garbled signals, all being transmitted from some threshold that is the imagined projection of our perception. In writing so as to tune out particular frequencies while tuning in to others, one reads—if by reading it can be taken to mean that a number of signals, fragments of otherwise irreparably lost wavelengths, are gathered into some meaningful pattern, however much one might believe that one is simply reporting or recording, or however minimally one strives to interpret the information in question. The writer who is also a reader, and a reader not only of those fragments but also of what he or she writes in order to project an image of the historical moment, constructs an image, however fractured or ruptured. The image of representation that comes to be projected and enacted is the result of piecing together many smaller images, representations, and details ripped from the time of their previous inscriptions, and subsequently transmitted across time. What one reads, and the traces that one translates in the act of writing, thus presents itself in any analysis already mired in layer upon layer of archival reading and writing. Playing on the editorial fiction, the archivist who orders those documents referred to in the title of the novel as *posthumous,* Dickens deterritorializes any authority in the very act of narration. Thus *The Posthumous Papers of the Pickwick Club* allows us to apprehend the textual lines of flight, its constellated interanimations of discourses and tropes, and its rhizomic field of forces, all of which come together in the production of re-presentation, of vision as revision.

What *does* take place therefore in any manifestation of textual becoming is inescapably a "rhetorical inquiry," to employ Regenia Gagnier's phrase; this inquiry in turn is comprehended as "the analysis of a particular set of circumstances, the judgements made thereof, and the persuasion to accept the judgement and its appropriate action, and it is centrally concerned with value" (1991, 4). Thus, in directing you to what cannot help but be a highly selective number of events, documents, or practices (whether material or discursive), I am both making a judgement and inviting you to accept that judgement, much like "Boz," the fictional and therefore phantasmic, apparitional "editor" of *Pickwick*. And even while I remark that all such practices are provisional, marked by chance, it is also doubtless that I am, to a degree, imbuing a chance concatenation of disparate elements, the signs of which remain available and communicate in some manner today, with both significance and meaning. There are both forensic and deliberative processes at work in the rhetorical inquiry, and these take place "in the elaboration of a nonreductionist understanding of cultures," as Gagnier has it (1991, 6).

Thus the "past," "history," "events," all are names for what Gagnier calls "a particular set of circumstances." Or, to put this another way, such names provide provisional rather than fixed labels for a network or, again, a constellation of relations that are profoundly textual in their interconnectedness. The literary is always this weaving and unweaving of "a particular set of circumstances," whether those circumstances or events are wholly imagined or "based on historical events" and subsequently fictionalized and re*vis*ed; the literary is always *just this* mesh of *circumstances* and their becoming visible. These are textual inasmuch as we do not read "moments" or "events" in isolation from one another. And they are textual, moreover, inasmuch as what we do when we think we read is both forensic and determinative, it is analytical and therefore caught up in a process of translation, as well as one of reception. The "past," so called, has in fact already undergone a translation effect, as I have remarked; for it is never recuperable as such, as others experienced it, and, it has to be said, as every one of those others experienced it differently. What takes place is the impossibility of witnessing as its only possibility, as the reader is confronted with an experience of the aporetic. Dickens offers an acute and ironic focus on the encounter with the undecidable in the prosopopoeic yet invisible experience of Boz. When one considers the effect of *Pickwick*'s so-called editor on the reader, as I do in chapter 3, there are occasions when both frustration and amusement are engendered. On several occasions Boz remarks that knowledge is undecidable, that no authoritative commentary can be made on the basis of the textual evidence, which is supposed to stand in for, and to supplement, the material, historical event. Beyond the frustration of the reader and the comedy at both the reader's and the narrated subject's expense, there may come to be seen, and so read, an indirect commentary on the ethical problem bearing witness to what cannot be experienced as such. Through this performative re-presentation of the aporia of reading, and envisioning, of the past, Boz reproduces and so reiterates for the reader's experience the editorial or archival experience. And this is produced, do not forget, *with a difference,* thereby attesting to the differential structure that simultaneously opens to view the traces of the past in the act of representation while calling to mind the particular set of circumstances as a rhetorical moment of becoming.

V. Deciphering and Self-Reading

Clearly from all that I have said there can be no doubt that no work of literature is produced in a vacuum. No text arrives without the signs of its histories, its cultures, its ideologies. This is well known. However, this being the case, there is also no direct one-to-one correlation, and neither is the cultural relationship of text and context static. A text will bear the signs of being overdetermined by many other historical and cultural moments (see, for example, my discussion of the phrase "diminishing glass," as found in Dickens' *The Pickwick Papers*). To recall again one of my epigraphs, Thomas Carlyle admits as much when he observes the following: "To *combine* any *picture* of these University, and subsequent, years; much more, to *decipher* therein any *illustrative* primordial elements of the Clothes-philosophy, becomes such a problem as the reader may imagine. So much we can *see;* darkly, as through the foliage of some wavering thicket" (emphasis added). The italics illustrate telegraphically and, as it were, in an encrypted fashion the intimate relation between verbal and visual codes. Carlyle's consideration of reconstructing a past in *Sartor Resartus* presents us with the problem of writing and reading historical events in narrative form and the problems attendant on the production of a vision of that past, in a nutshell. Historically, it might be said, with one eye on the past and the other on the present, all we can see is that, in attempting to produce a representation in the present that is clear, we see that we cannot see that well. Thus, Carlyle is happy to inform us, we read ourselves reading our own historical myopia, and without a very clear view of how to proceed. Yet if, as I argue, Dickens' text offers a moment of self-reading of particular middle-class English identities, as these, in turn, come into an awareness of themselves in the first third of the nineteenth century, we may begin to see a strategy for proceeding in the singular vision of self-reading.

Self-reading is more than simply self-representation, although it may, on an initial glance, bear similarities to and even begin from a process of reflection as identification. Self-reading is, it might be said, the process of a deconstructive opening from within self-representation, in which an other reading begins, an other reading and a reading of the other; in short, an act of reading in excess of the reflection situated in self-representation. In such a mode of perception that is merely reflective the reader may view oneself as "an agent for whom perception is a holding onto things . . . and thus a means of maintaining oneself in the world" (Vasseleu 1998, 66). Such envisioning is comforting: for if I believe I see similarity, or even sameness, in those who, though no longer alive, share in the past my cultural identity, and therefore see in myself the possibility of a pure repetition or continuation of that identity, I apprehend the future possibility that after my death there will be others just like me. However, self-reading, which relies on a certain obliquity of vision, extends and overflows reflective representation. For, while perception of partial resemblance is necessary there is within that "contiguous touching" (Vasseleu 1998, 66) a discontinuity. The image I envision of the other is a representation, a re-presentation, which, in being marked visibly by difference, is apprehended as the same and yet not the same. In perceiving this, self-reading operates in—and as—a "mode of sensibility, which, in maintaining itself, parts company" (Vasseleu 1998, 66) from the intangible-visible, one's memory of the other and the past. With that other reading there is the chance—though never more than this—of perceiving an other vision, and with it a glimpse of the other. While self-representation may be critical or, at least, a critique of social and historical self, such a critical stance can still be generated from the same ideological or philosophical positions as the identity being held up for critique and hence produce or illuminate blind spots that are, themselves, the signs of a particular text's historicity. Thus the language of criticism and the object of the critique circulate within the same economy of identity. Self-reading interrupts and moves beyond the merely critical; at least, in principle, this is what it should do. In this movement I would argue that implicit representation of the self as marked by difference is the sign of an inauguration of modernity; and modernity's coming into being is inaugurated, since the eighteenth century at least, by "the passage to self-representation," both ontologically and philosophically (Colebrook 1999, 1).

However, the idiosyncrasy, the singularity of *Pickwick*'s modernity is that it re-marks its singularly "modern" condition through an archival becoming that, like Benjamin's Angel of History, moves forward while facing backward, bearing the traces of remembrance and a condition of being haunted, as I shall explore in the final chapter. Through often satirical or parodic gestures and visions of cultural self-reading, *Pickwick* moves beyond the merely critical, unveiling otherwise "invisible" cultural and ideological habit and convention. It achieves this through its constant exploration of the comedic possibilities of representation, and the crisis within the visible to which comedy gives us access. In so doing, it brings the immaterial motion of such habits to light in their material manifestations as so many structures or cultural institutions given intense scrutiny, put under the magnifying lens of the critical microscope or pen. It is through the satirical and parodic, the farcical and lampooned, that we have the chance—though, again, never more than this—of coming to *see* (in both senses) that "there can be no knowledge of things in themselves. To be known or experienced a thing must be other than the knower; it must be *given* to the knower. As *known,* things are only as they are re-presented to a subject" (Colebrook 1999, 2). Yet when the mediating subject is the editor, Boz; and when that editor repeatedly affirms undecidability in the face of the limits of the knowledge being presented and represented; then representation itself, the image, envisioning, etc.—all are the visible signs of what Claire Colebrook calls the "recognition of knowledge's position, limit, *point of view* and, most importantly, its *separation*" by which modernity comes into being (Colebrook 1999, 2; first emphasis mine). Such processes of separation, along with instances of discontinuity within representation, supplementarity, and difference, are readable as necessary facets in the work of self-reading. They produce, and are traced in, a double vision that is peculiar to the novel, as we shall have occasion to see from several perspectives. Through its various types of vision, and its invitations to its reader to consider *how we see,* while coming to see that we only see in a mediated and indirect manner, *The Posthumous Papers of the Pickwick Club* becomes available to the good reader as offering a timely, and yet untimely, anachronistic and haunting reminder of the importance of a certain vigilance having to do with memory, bearing witness, and maintaining the signs of the past, while looking to that which is to come.

1

History's Difference

That a Picture painted in its utmost degree of Perfection, ought so to affect the Eye of the Beholder, that he should not be able to judge, whether what he sees be only a few Colours laid artificially on a Cloth, or the very Objects there represented, seen thro' the Frame of the Picture, as thro' a Window. . . . To produce this Effect, it is plain the Light ought to come from the Picture to the Spectator's Eye. . . .
—Brook Taylor, *Linear Perspective, or, a new method of representing justly all manner of Objects as they appear to the Eye in all situations* (1715)

An entire epoch of so-called literature, if not all of it, cannot survive a certain technological regime of telecommunications.
—Jacques Derrida, *The Post Card: From Socrates to Freud and Beyond* (1980)

[*Pickwick*'s] generic looseness—is it a novel, or isn't it?—has left some modern readers uncomfortable.
—Paul Schlicke, *Oxford Reader's Companion to Dickens* (1999)

I. Novel Differences, or "Signatures of the Age"

"Admirers of *Pickwick Papers,*" John Bowen tells us, "have often seen it as a beginning like no other . . . an inaugurative creative act" (2000, 49). In a hyperbolic gesture recalling the opening sentence of Dickens' *The Posthumous Papers of the Pickwick Club,* Steven Marcus avers that *Pickwick* "dramatizes the fundamental activity of the Logos" (1987, 133). What, though, if anything, was *inventive,* if not exactly *new,* or say instead *novel,* about *Pickwick*? How do we situate ourselves with regard to *The Pickwick Papers* so as to perceive, however indirectly, its difference? In the current chapter, I shall attempt to trace a number of networks concerning the material conditions of *Pickwick*'s becoming, along with subsequent views of the novel's identity (and by extension the identity of Dickens, however briefly), prior to any discussion of the novel's poetics and mechanics of the visual in the chapters that follow.

To restore its full title, *The Posthumous Papers of the Pickwick Club containing a faithful record of the perambulations, perils, travels, adventures and Sporting Transactions of the corresponding members. Edited by "Boz"* was written and published in serial form (in monthly installments) between 1836 and 1837, when Dickens was twenty-four. Though it was to become Dickens' first novel, it was not his first book, this being *Sketches by Boz,* a collection of loosely associated "scenes" of contemporary London life. In addition, Charles Dickens had already published (and continued to write throughout the rest of his career) reviews, essays, reports, and other journalistic sketches.[1]

From its inception in March 1836, when advertisements were placed by publishers Chapman and Hall announcing the serial publication, *Pickwick* was an "experiment" (*PP* xi), as the editor of the Penguin edition, Mark Wormald, remarks. The experiment lay in the publishers' *invention* of an apparently "new" periodical. *Pickwick* was, however, not a new periodical. It was not a magazine or journal in which was included either the serialization of old established novels or diluted commentaries on recent scientific advances. It merely had the appearance of being such a publication. It "masquerad[ed] as a serious periodical" (*PP* xii) in an era of "miscellanies, accessible collections," a period when "weekly and monthly magazines and papers took few risks" (*PP* xi). In producing *The Pickwick Papers,* Dickens employed his editorial persona, Boz. In doing so, he drew on "the traditional novelist's device of constructing a fictional editor" by which Dickens "align[ed] himself with the likes of Walter Scott" and others (Grossman 1997, 180), as we will have occasion to discuss in the next section of this chapter. Additionally, however, Dickens "also "construct[ed] his own beginning as a novelist" through the novelty of a "verbose editor who [was] at once a parody of Dickens and yet Dickens the parodist" (Grossman 1997, 180). So: an instance of doubling, and a duplication within that—for the fiction of the editor that occludes the figure of the author also allows for that author to parody both the function and "voice" of the editor, while also imitating himself (imitating himself, as it were). Through the mimicry of tradition an ironic self-distancing inscription, which is also a self-reading, takes place in the construction and role of the inscribing/inscribed subject. The inscription of literary tradition and convention as the sign of a distancing, self-aware parody is further figured through the title. The alliteration of the full title was an aural and graphic reminder of other publications, designed to call to mind the image of the familiar and comforting; yet in its echoes of that familiarity it also drew attention to the mechanisms by which comfort was generated. *Pickwick* was a simulacrum of the "real thing," and one that anticipated and wagered on a readership eager to respond not to novelty but a publication bearing all the signs of familiarity and tradition. Such a simultaneous registration of novelty and tradition, of innovation being *invented* within the conventional, was clearly a means of an equally simultaneous inscription of remembering and forgetting, of tracing "unlikeness" through an acknowledgment of resemblance in the imitation and mimicry of form, and therefore identity. As Mark Wormald asks, "how better to signal your own proper distance from a world whose passing you half regretted than by laughing at someone's slightly ridiculous heartiness?" (*PP* xi).

As is well known, this *faux* periodical was originally intended as a vehicle for the popular caricaturist Robert Seymour (1800–1836), who specialized in sporting scenes. Seymour himself had proposed to the publishers a series of illustrations of Cockney sporting life at the end of 1835.[2] However, as readers of Dickens will be equally aware, almost from the beginning of publication Dickens argued with Chapman and Hall that the story, not the illustrations, should provide the principal focus, and following the second serial part Seymour had a nervous breakdown, dying shortly thereafter having provided illustrations for the first five chapters only, leaving the fate and adventures of the Pickwick club in Dickens' hands. Initially replacing Seymour was R. W. Buss, whose work was also unsatisfactory as far as Dickens was concerned. He was subsequently replaced by Hablot Knight Browne, who was, in the guise of "Phiz" to Dickens' "Boz," to remain Dickens' principal illustrator for more than twenty years. Following the death of Robert Seymour, Dickens swiftly inaugurated a number of changes to format, doing away with Seymour's original idea of the adventures of a sporting club (one of the familiar forms of periodical entertainment), and producing a monthly publication that went from a length of twenty-four pages with four illustrations to thirty-two pages with two illustrations. It would surely not be going too far to suggest that in the decision to reduce the number of illustrations, Dickens clearly believed that what the reader would come to *see* in the mind's eye was a more powerful vision than any merely material image; for the phantasm projected in response to the words on the page would be generated by memory and feeling, and would therefore take on a more singular force for every reader.

Of course, serial publication of fiction was not a new phenomenon in the 1830s, as we have implied. Literary magazines had conventionally serialized fiction. Novels such as Sir Walter Scott's *Waverly,* which had already been published in volume form, were serialized with much success. *Pickwick* was, however, a significant publication in that in its arrival on the publishing scene it presented the world with a wholly new story, one not seen previously in volume form, and thus untried, untested. At first contemporary reviewers were fully taken in by the periodical as the genuine item, as Kathryn Chittick has shown (1984, 328–35). *Pickwick* was reviewed not as a novel but as a magazine, reviewers accepting as real the fictive Boz as compiler of disparate sources. With its initially "wandering and almost plotless form" that "revel[led] in a fluid and fragmentary life, acknowledging only the temporary unity of vignettes" (Grossman 1997, 173, 175), *Pickwick* began and was accepted as an oddity, "a periodical, with only one article" (Chittick 1984, 335).

However, as Dickens assumed control of both the story and, effectively, the publication, the structuring of the narrative gradually became more coherent and continuous, thereby becoming a *novel* and a *novelty,* a *novel novel* as it were.[3] It was thus the combination of familiarity of narrative type—*Pickwick*'s initial indebtedness in the choice of material to stories of sporting men's clubs, along with other sources—with the risk taken in publishing unprinted material in serial form that came to have a marked effect on the commissioning of new works initially for the serial market, both for Dickens and other nineteenth-century novelists, as we are informed by Jonathan Grossman, in an article on representation and the law courts (1997, 171–97) in *Pickwick,* and by Peter Ackroyd in his biography of Dickens (1990, 180). As Grossman puts it, "*Pickwick* . . . usher[ed] in a new era in the serialization of novels. With *Pickwick,* for the first time a serial begins drawing on the material that an author is producing month by month. . . . *Pickwick* itself is news" (1997, 171). A hypothesis then: such novelty may itself have had an effect on the identity of the novel. For, as Kathryn Chittick argues, *Pickwick* demonstrates—indeed performs—the internal, narrative transformation of the novel in its foregrounding of hybridity, fragmentation, and the intimation that "the novel, as Dickens improvised it, may follow the principle of a miscellany" (Chittick 1984, 335). Thus, we come to see the novel-in-ruins, as it were, as the visible symptom and expression of literary modernity in the nineteenth century. In intervening in the market in this singular manner, Dickens marks the practice of fiction writing in a particularly striking way, one that is not simply a moment of transformation but also one that knowingly departs from conventional modes of fiction's dissemination. Similarly, the reception of fiction was also transformed, and not merely for the reading public. Serialization led to more rapid and widespread reviewing than had been customary for novels appearing in volume form. Dickens and his publishers turned the conventions and the institutions of serial publication on their heads, doing so not with a markedly "new" type of tale, but writing a tale greatly indebted to earlier forms of narrative (*the old stories*). Why insist on this point? The *chance* concatenation of old and new, established practice and departure from accepted perceptions of the market traverses *The Pickwick Papers* from extrinsic factors of publication—and success—to internal processes of adherence to and parody or satire of narrative modes and conventions.

I insist on *chance* because the last thing I wish to imply is that there is something wholly deliberate, or concerted, taking place. What is observed is very much the imposition of a strong reading that ranges from the economic to the ideological, from culture to aesthetics. But this strong reading allows us to *see* Dickens' novel retrospectively, to perceive with hindsight its particular moment of appearance, not in isolation but as the accidental manifestation of a range of cultural, ideological, and aesthetic forces. It might even be argued that the publication of an entirely new story in a recognized and established mode of production, one that bears all the signs—however satirized or parodied—of earlier narrative forms, marks and may be viewed as what Paul Ricoeur describes as "the entry of memory into the public sphere" through the specific act of making visible for a mass market a range of "phenomena of identification" (2004, 129) simultaneously commensurate with and dislocated from earlier manifestations of Englishness. Form is unlikeness; every difference is form.

The very modes of production just illustrated—material, ideological, aesthetic, and formal—by which *Pickwick* comes into material being and by which it signs its cultural moment through *becoming visible* exemplifies some of the more general arguments concerning the novel and the tropes of vision that I have already explored in the introduction. From the start, we might say, we come to perceive how identity is both disrupted and invented. This is *Pickwick*'s vision, and it is through the gap that the novel opens in identity that we come to glimpse this vision, as well as how the vision is structured and inscribed materially. To insist on this point, Dickens' inaugural novel, in both its narrative forms and the forms of its appearance on the literary scene, is informed simultaneously by tradition *and* innovation. It bears a double signature, displaying the signs of historical indebtedness *and* that modernity of which I have spoken in the introduction: on the one hand, a distancing, self-aware representation of the *novel* as a form of reiteration; and on the other, the *novelty* of re-presentation through iterability.

To reiterate: such "novelty" announces itself internally through the narrative's estranging pastiche of the old. In this a gap is opened to our gaze between old and new, then and now; this breach is readable as the articulation of a cultural consciousness mediating the moment of its coming into being. A forceful *après-coup* to earlier and contemporary periodicals and narrative forms *as well as* a belated expression of such tales through the illusion of editorial anamnesis, *Pickwick* is simultaneously inventive *and* translative, *institutive* and *conservative* (Derrida 1996a, 7). It is, in effect, and in the scene of its re-presentation, a cultural *roman à clef,* staging a moment of being English, enacting a bourgeois identity in its becoming. It offers a number of countersignatures to all the impressions left on it, and to which it responds, by those other fictional forms and material publications. The countersignatures in turn inaugurate and authorize a double economics—of forgetting *and* anamnesis. In this they affirm themselves through the difference by which they come to be articulated as what Benjamin calls the "signatures of the age" (2002a, 139). An archiving of the literary (as we shall see), *Pickwick* is also, in effect, a "capitalization on [cultural] memory" (Derrida 1996a, 12) in an epoch when English middle-class identity is striving to mark its distance from earlier manifestations of that memory. Moreover, *Pickwick*'s narrative, aesthetic capitalization serves to make its mode of publishing a "capitalization" also, whereby "art comes into contact with the commodity; the commodity comes into contact with art" (Benjamin 2002b, 143). In this, the traces of earlier literary and aesthetic forms that *Pickwick* reproduces with a difference offer the comic distraction of distanciation from the form being parodied. What the novel finds within itself as other than itself, and what it effectively deterritorializes historically, it reterritorializes through the force of the materiality of its historical moment. However, such reterritorialization is never entirely effective. For the traces of the other leave a visible impression to resonate, to echo, and to haunt from within the present moment, as any good reader of *A Christmas Carol* will be aware—and which every critic intent on misreading will misread under the signs of transcendent redemption or sentiment. Neither present nor past is privileged explicitly but the temporal gap between the two becomes visible through the transformation of the trace of memory.

There is to be read, then, a doubleness involving an act of writing (and reading) and seeing oneself within the institution of literature and textual transmission, concerning which there will be more to say. As Jonathan Grossman has averred, *Pickwick* arrives through a doubling in representation, in which "differences define and maintain each other," for *The Posthumous Papers of the Pickwick Club* "takes its own representations and even its own authorship as its subject through [the effects of a doubling] displacement" (Grossman 1997, 176). The doubleness being addressed here multiplies itself in various ways. Not merely an effect of formal intertextual relations (though this is undeniably a significant aspect of its reduplications), it touches intimately on the very nature of perception and memory, and on any phenomenological registration of the reception and diffusion of manifestations of the visible throughout the novel. For now, though, we will turn to that which comes to be seen through the historicity of the intertextual, and the shuttle between the textual moment and the traces of its others.

II. Historicity's Difference

Dominic Rainsford has suggested that while it "is unlikely that Dickens saw any of Blake's Prophetic Books . . . the Blake-like imagery of Dickens's concluding sentence [to the preface of the Cheap Edition of *Pickwick*] signifies a shared Biblical and radical heritage, and a shared disposition towards the grandly metaphorical" (Rainsford 1997, 105).[4] Harry Stone, on the other hand, has commented of *Pickwick*'s election scenes, that they are, "among many things, rethought and reworked versions of the four satiric scenes in [William Hogarth's] *The Election*" of 1755–1758 (1994, 50–51). The melodrama of the grotesquely satirical in Hogarth's scenes serves to inform a hyperbolic satire, which in its own way serves to produce a textual effect equivalent to that of "grandly metaphorical" millenarian vision. Such vision and such satire are all too easily misread in Dickens as reactionary, overly emotional, or on occasion sentimental, a retreat from clear political or historical vision. However, as Stone goes on to make clear, the Dickensian process of textual anamnesis, of putting to work cultural and social memories and their traces, is one also of translation; the visions that appear on the page bear the indelible signs of both past times *and* the cultural moment of envisioning as re-visioning. The act of doubling and displacement is marked therefore by an intertextual and formal difference that is also the articulation of the text's historicity. Hogarth is not the only artist who leaves his trace on the modes of representation in *The Pickwick Papers,* though. Sterne, Smollett, Sheridan, Cervantes—as is familiar to many readers of Dickens, these and other authors provided Dickens with sources for the transformation and reformulation, the production of images, visions, narrative structures, and the occasionally reinvented citation, which, though bearing the traces of his paternal ghosts, nonetheless, come to be re-marked with a difference.[5] The comparison between Mr Pickwick and Don Quixote is a long-standing one, amongst the first to remark this being Washington Irving in a letter to Dickens in 1841, with subsequent remarks made notably by Edgar Johnson and W. H. Auden (see McMaster 1983, 595).

Reading *Pickwick*'s indebtedness to his literary precursors, Alexander Welsh also comments on the Pickwick-Quixote resemblance, observing that Mr Pickwick would have been immediately recognizable to many of the serial's readers as a nineteenth-century Don Quixote, with Sam Weller his Sancho Panza (Welsh 1967–68, 19–20). However, this resonance, while significant as the sign of Dickens' personal literary inheritance, can also be read for its difference, as well as its resemblance, thereby causing to become visible the traces of ideological inflection and the material conditions by which the temporal moment comes to be traced. As Edward Said has remarked, "whatever work is, in fact, produced, is haunted by antecedence, difference, sameness, and the future" (1975, 227), all of which we shall have occasion to see at work in different ways in the various examples on which I draw in this study.

What comes to be revealed in the comparison between the two literary figures, albeit indirectly—looking, as it were, at the imagined Victorian reader reading this resemblance—is, in the early nineteenth century, a matter of the articulation of class relations. As N. N. Feltes has it in his materialist analysis of *Pickwick* as commodity-text (in serial form it sold some forty thousand copies a month at the height of its success[6]), the "significance of the relationship between Mr. Pickwick and Sam lies . . . in its representation of an aspect of early Victorian England's *way of seeing itself*" (1986, 15–16; emphasis added). While I would be wary of the implied homogeneity, that monocular vision or representation, of Victorian England inscribed in "itself" (and, below, in the phrase *Victorian sense of self*), nevertheless, I concur entirely with the sentiment. For what it serves to illustrate or illuminate for Feltes is that "the implied parallel between Mr. Pickwick and Don Quixote . . . *together with* the difference in class and historical period, interpellate that specifically bourgeois Victorian sense of self" (16). The acknowledgment of intertextual reference, far from being merely formal or aesthetic, allows for and admits of another perspective to come into view, by a kind of anamorphic reading, the sideways glance or gesture of refraction I announce in the introduction. We are given a sidelong glimpse at how some readers of Dickens could be understood to be self-readers or, at least to glean anamorphically, analogically, a sense of selfhood in the early nineteenth century. Indeed, we apprehend how *Pickwick* is understandable as an act of self-reading involving the play of historical, ideological, and cultural differences between the Spain of Quixote and the England of Pickwick. Such play in *Pickwick* produces an image of early nineteenth-century class relations in the novel, which, while "haunted" (to use Said's word) by its literary antecedent, *works* precisely because it offers a representation that is traced by, as it mediates, its own historicity.

The modalities by which the signs of the historical are encrypted in any novel are undeniably complex. Arguably, when the form of the novel as developed by Dickens is a hybrid and heterogeneous miscellany, then the complexity of encryption is all the more profound as John Frow has argued (1986, 163). Dickens' fictive device of assigning the narrator the guise of an editor ("Boz") of *The Posthumous Papers of the Pickwick Club* who compiles, translates, and reorders innumerable and otherwise unreadable texts admits as much. Or, rather say that through the illusion of the ontological affirmation of his "being," that "he" is just this: a singular articulation of the complex hybrid that privileges discourse over the assumption of what Frow calls that quasi-real entity we envision as a "character" (161).[7]

Pausing a moment to digress briefly around the construction of Pickwick and how he sees the world through the sideways glances offered by the "editor-effect" in *Pickwick:* The perspective on the constitution of character afforded by Frow informs us directly about the editorial work of Boz in its attention to the novel's modes of focalization. Coming to see how Pickwick does not see, and especially that he does not see himself, is important in the act of self-reading. Hypothetically Mr Pickwick, "himself a kind of camera eye" (Miller 1958, 7), might see such a construction of self as historically given and therefore open to other perspectives and translations as "a dreadful conjunction of appearances" (*PP* 244), a remark made in reflection on how an event when seen is open to misconstrual despite *observation.* Boz might well respond, though, in the words of Mr Perker, "aye, aye . . . you can't be expected to *view* these subjects with a professional *eye*" (*PP* 401; emphasis added). There is a naïveté to Pickwick's belief in the scientific truth of empirical observation. Unlike Boz, he is unaware that there is an inescapably phenomenological, transformative dimension to sight and vision. Take, for example, Pickwick's response at Jingle's being paid off in return for giving up Miss Wardle (chapter 10):

> If any dispassionate spectator could have beheld the countenance of the illustrious man, whose name forms the leading feature of the title of this work . . . he would have been almost induced to wonder that the indignant fire which flashed from his eyes, did not melt the glasses of his spectacles. (*PP* 141–42)

Boz knowingly calls upon the reader's powers of visualization in a manner that invites the reader to step into the narrative, to step back in time metaphorically and so witness both the appearance of Mr Pickwick and his gaze. What the scene gives us is double: on the one hand it suspends narrative motion in favor of the time of visualization and the gaze; on the other hand, in being triggered from the position of an impossibility—the dispassionate spectator—the glance is seen to issue not from any subject as such, only the hypothesis of one. Thus the glance in its differentiated network gives itself in its phenomenal motivation to acknowledge that there is always the other's view. Boz's imaginative hypothesis draws attention to this through his own, otherwise invisible mediation of the scene, but it does so in order to direct our view to an eccentric place within the representation. As J. Hillis Miller has it, Pickwick "does not expect what he sees will involve or change himself" (1958, 7), but Boz sees that what is seen *does* transform the viewing subject emotionally (whether Pickwick in his anger or the reader through her laughter), and in such a way that the only appropriate, if comic, means of representing this is through the focus being directed to the act of looking; or more precisely, one gaze looking at another, and at yet another. For the reader must *see* the dispassionate *spectator,* who is not in fact there at all, looking at the metaphorical, and therefore not literally visible, appearance of fire, the displaced and volatile sign of indignation, as a result of Pickwick's particularly intense stare, the very power of which the editor imagines has the force to melt glass, thereby disabling clarity of vision in the very process of its magnification. Such a self-differencing and differentiating structure of vision, "in soliciting appearance," abandons the illusion of being issued from any stable representational point, and thus it "also relinquishes itself to appearance, and to being encountered by the other" (Fotí 2004, 82).

It is not simply that vision comes to be structured by language in *Pickwick* (although it does). Instead, *vision is structured like a language.* Reciprocally, language is not mimetic but apophantic,[8] the materiality of inscription lets something be seen appearing from itself. Boz would give us to *see* in both senses; if we just look carefully enough we will understand through what comes to appear. If we open our eyes and read, reading will open our eyes. In this play between the verbal and the visual the truth of vision is unfolded: every discussion of seeing, the gaze, vision and visibility in *Pickwick* is always about the structures of seeing and perception; *what* we see serves to offer the possibility to reflect on *how* we see, and representation opens us to consider how we are never dispassionate spectators, especially when it is a matter of seeing the past or seeing others. We can never gaze dispassionately because the structure of vision is always one that has anticipated our being enfolded, and so *seen* within it. Seeing thus comes to be seen as a fraught process, open to refraction, distortion, displacement, perhaps condensation, and possibly even blindness. How one sees—and so perceives the ways in which others see—is always open to misreading. If Dickens is "ready to be particularly generous to the eye" in *Pickwick,* as Juliet McMaster claims (1983, 597), such rhetorical and representational munificence has its consequences. Too much of a good thing can be bad for one, and so a vigilance has to be kept over sight and vision. The problem for Pickwick is, as James Marlow suggests, that he "reads literally and so loses *sight* . . . of the essential indeterminability" (1985, 946; emphasis added) produced by that difference which opens perspective from within itself, and which, moreover, one runs the risk of losing sight of as the gap opened between the time of the event and that of reading widens. If sight cannot be trusted, if it is in the process of going awry in the near-immediacy of its response to an event, as the passage above suggests, then what is to be trusted when what we see is subject to the displacements and duplications of temporal and interpretive relays? Literal reading and trusting to the veracity of one's optical powers is precisely what Boz calls into question, in a manner that invites us to question how we read and therefore see "character" and to understand, reflect on, our own role in that process. Thus Boz invites us to look at ourselves indirectly through looking at Pickwick (whose way of viewing the world comes to appear anachronistic), and therefore to see our temporal and cultural difference from him.

To look at this in two ways at once, as we had previously done with the reading of the comparison between Samuel Pickwick and Don Quixote: on the one hand, the assumption of an editorial function on the part of the author is one Dickens knowingly borrows from the past, from those authors with whom he is familiar, such as Scott or Smollett, Defoe or Richardson.[9] Thus *Pickwick* is haunted by a particular mode of narrative production taken from the tradition of English fiction. In being employed by Dickens in the 1830s, the function of the editor no longer has the same historical or cultural significance it once had. Yet, to read the difference that is at work in this self-conscious and self-reflexive borrowing, the purpose of the fictive editor is to reveal how, from a materialist perspective, *Pickwick* is not merely the production of its author, but is also a publication that takes place "within a determinate subensemble of emerging industrial capitalism, the production of written texts" (Feltes 1986, 3). Moreover, one sees the construct of the editor as a semivisible figure who, on the one hand, causes to appear those other characters and figures, such as Pickwick or Sam Weller, and, on the other, gives us the possibility to perceive the difference and historicity of such production, while also demonstrating on occasion *how* looking brings about change. For the difference between the editor effect in *Pickwick* and that produced through those "editors" preceding and informing the constitution of Boz is summed up thus, by J. Hillis Miller. It becomes possible for us to see that "if there is any essential change in the characters [in *Pickwick*]," as Miller has it, "it is primarily *in our apprehension* of them" (1958, 26; emphasis added) rather than in any "internal" transformation. And it is through that which the editor *chooses* to let the reader see of his characters' limited changes of apprehension—unlike the "inalterable permanence of characters" of the eighteenth-century novel (Miller 1958, 27)—that we come to perceive the historical difference in representation.

This far from exhausts the reading of the editor function or effect, which from such a perspective we might also apprehend, and thus name, a *subensemble* of culturally and ideologically determined and interpellated practices. What can be said for now, however, is that this reading serves to offer a glimpse at the ways in which particular material and historical traces come to be encoded within a single figure or identity. As with the Don Quixote–Sancho Panza commentary, the doubling of the editorial fiction or effect is read from within the text itself. We come to see something taking place intrinsically, not from two separate locations but from within one place. Markedly historical (the historicity of the trace comes into focus through what one might term the binocular reading), the double resonances in question disrupt and suspend how one views and therefore gives ontological or historical meaning to a text. It is *as if* what John Frow describes, in his readings of *Little Dorrit* (1855–57) and *Our Mutual Friend* (1864–65), as that "internal contradiction" that places a text "outside the representational mainstream" (1986, 166), insists that we consider matters of perspective, viewpoint, focus, and other visual concerns in questioning the very notion of representation. In minute ways, Dickens suspends the movement of his narrative in *Pickwick* and causes us to focus differently through references to railways and gas microscopes, technologies not properly in existence during the 1820s, and certainly not comprehensible or visible in the ways that they will become just a decade later.

Let us take one small example, being illustrative, as Boz might say, of the opening of sight to its temporal disruption to which I have just referred. My example is the title of chapter 8: "Strongly illustrative of the Position, that the course of true love is not a Railway" (*PP* 107). As is well known, the title is a translation of a citation from *A Midsummer Night's Dream.* As with all titles and citations, there is an effort to give the tone to the chapter, obviously. But in observing the translation, with its overwriting of the citation, the title becomes visible—if one *sees* the quotation—as a palimpsest of sorts. What is given is in more than one tone. In its work a strange, comic temporal and cultural disjointing is put to work by the title. Shakespeare is partially rewritten, but a remnant of late sixteenth-century culture remains visible here, surviving beyond its cultural moment despite the arrival of the technology in the form of the railway. Yet Shakespeare survives only in ruins, the railway being a violent intrusion on the cultural and imaginary landscape. Another more subtle dislocation is also produced, for while the novel is written and published in 1836–37, its events take place a decade earlier, as I have already noted. Mr Pickwick cannot know of railways, at least not as a form of commercial public transport. While we might pass over this, it should be borne in mind that the narrator seeks to draw attention to what takes place here through that figure of visible representation, *illustration,* while there is a further oddity here inasmuch as there is an equation between the verbal passage of the chapter and the implication of the title that through the passage of language something will come to be *seen.* The force of the chapter is in its being illustrative of, and therefore a supplement to, the title's aphoristic affirmation despite the obvious absence of any train. The title wields the still novel—for the reader—technology of the railway as a somewhat violent anticipation of that illustration, and the temporal displacement that is implicitly effected is quite startling, if one pauses to look at it. We will only have come to *see* the truth of the title *after* we have read the chapter, a chapter in which it is doubtless needless to remark that the railway is spectacular by its absence (as, indeed, is Shakespeare). But if my statement appears merely an example of weakly comic hyperbole, is that not in fact the point here? What is absent, virtually nonexistent—as anachronistic in its own fashion as the phantom mail coach appearing later in chapter 48—has all the more force as phantasmic illustration arriving from the future of the narrative at a moment when it has become *posthumous.*

History, we might say, is what has past and what is to come, but like the time of reading it is never locatable now. What we *see* if we look carefully in *Pickwick,* if we give attention to the act of looking and the vision or visions entailed therein, are sights incommensurate with any straightforward historical or factual presentation or representation. As *The Pickwick Papers* appears to intimate in various ways, however representation comes to takes place, its projection is always internally contested by various material and historical currents. In addition, the grounds of identity or meaning, in being materially given and overdetermined, are always multiple, unstable, and ultimately undecidable. That which constitutes either the "tone" of a title or the meaning of *identity* or *being*—whether this is figured through the notion of the "editor" or a character such as Mr Pickwick—involves the circulation and recirculation of material and cultural events, traces, and discourses in a complex network of interrelations. There are other forms of cultural and historical transmission that, unconfined to any one historical epoch, shape identity, in invisible ways, and which, coming together, construct being in various cultural, communal, or social manifestations—which then are ontologized through the application of terms such as "Victorian" or "national identity"—as overdetermined. Such overdetermination, in taking place in complex and heterogeneous ways, when brought to light and viewed closely, may often appear paradoxical, and irresolvable into any simple, single, or homogeneous identity.

One aspect of such paradoxical doubling, and with that the difference or alterity emerging from within the possibility of identity or identification, is the recognition of that simultaneous proximity and distance already announced, marked by the decade between the novel's imaginary events and the remainders of its resonance in the editorial transcription of the posthumous papers. *The Pickwick Papers* situates its adventures over the course of some eighteen months. Its narrative is located historically in the years 1827–28. Indeed, *Pickwick* is precise about its starting date, 12 May 1827 (*PP* 15). Such an act of dating, as observable as is the fleeting appearance of a train where no train should be, draws our attention to itself in its visible and graphic precision. Such graphic gesture doubles the temporal moment and thereby remarks its own place between two materialities, that of the material event and that of the inscribed, translated memory. This is, in itself, a further reduplication, inasmuch as Boz's editorial work reiterates not the Pickwickian moment but the earlier inscription of that moment in those posthumous papers. If we look closely we perceive that, busily at work, Boz is the spectator who helps to make possible the projection of the image. He is the witness, not to the events either in themselves or as such, but to the traces of those historical instances, and through these to other ghostly spectators, whose only signs of witness are those documents signed by various hands and announced as "posthumous." James Marlow has observed (1985, 939) that Boz, the self-advertising "editor of these papers" (*PP* 15), refers to "the secretary, to whose notes we are indebted" (*PP* 16). As Marlow suggests, the act of writing is foregrounded in this; but there is also to be understood a question of envisioning. Such auto-reflexivity on the part of Boz invites the reader to "see" the very figure who, though leaving his mark everywhere throughout the text, cannot be seen. However, again to cite Marlow: "every episode supposedly bears the traces of at least two mediators" (939). There is no possibility of unmediated vision, particularly when one is referring to the past; the present is only ever the passing away of the trace that affirms the opening of the gap that makes possible perception of the difference between the moment of inscription and that which the materiality of the letter seeks to re-represent. This affirmation of material difference and the haunting force of the trace of historicity announce *Pickwick*'s modernity, as well as the source of much of its comedy.

That relay described as "focalization" in the introduction is thus always under way. Into this structure and the lacunae and discontinuities by which it is structured, we are introduced. The result is that what is immeasurably distant and otherwise invisible comes to appear, and appears to be seen, with a deceptively easy intimacy. However, imagining just for the instant ourselves as the first readers of *Pickwick*, we come to see ourselves in 1837 as relatively close to the events of the novel and its characters, though we are not their contemporaries; and neither are they ours, not quite. There is an unclosable gap. If *Pickwick* is slightly displaced, though, neither is it absolutely "historical." It remarks its doubling through its resistance to, and overflow from, any stable ontology. It is not a novel that offers a representation of "the way we live now." Nor does it offer a simple representation or naïve view of the past as irrevocably past. *Pickwick* is not a "historical novel" like either *Barnaby Rudge* or *A Tale of Two Cities,* set in another period markedly dissimilar from the time of writing. In *Pickwick,* however, a small temporal shift has occurred that draws our attention to the matter of narrative, historicity, and an apparent historically specific embeddedness, which relies nonetheless, and despite the gap that is opened, upon a readerly perception of the familiarity of the trace. *Pickwick*'s proximity *and* distance apropos the past thus serves as a peculiar, singular manifestation of the nineteenth-century obsession with the material conditions of ontological apprehension, reflection, and perception. Its singularity is signalled, arguably, in its insistence that, however ruined, however irrevocably past, the past never leaves us and informs both being and identity, whether personally or to a greater cultural extent.

III. Are We Feeling Historically Yet? or, Modes of Perception

As should be clear, temporal doubling or, at least, oscillation within the reader's field of vision with regard to the traces of the past effects a disturbance in any supposedly stable present moment (once again), and, crucially for this study, the means of representation of such an event and any experience of that. Doubling, division, iterability—the effects of each are registered in *Pickwick* through the attention to vision and the visible, and moreover, in the shaping of reading. This doubling process is markedly cultural, social, and material, not to say historical; and, in the words of Raymond Williams on the occlusion of feeling, experience, and subjectivity in certain Marxist critical discourses, "it is the reduction of the social to fixed forms that remains the basic error" (Williams 1977, 129), and which attention to the trope of the visual overcomes in its fluidity. As we shall have occasion to observe at the end of this chapter and then again, in more sustained fashion in the final chapter of *The Old Story, with a Difference,* feeling historically is closely connected to the matter of vision, and is connected closely moreover to the sentimental and the grandly metaphorical. But to return to doubling, the motion of replication/division/iteration informs and reveals *how* the reader is invited or directed to see in any crucial moment within that which Kevis Goodman defines as "the flux of historical process" (2004, 3). For example, we are confronted directly with one material aspect of the past, when there appear before us "some half dozen old inns, which have preserved their external features unchanged," forgotten along the "improved streets of London" and occluded "amidst the modern innovations that surround them" (*PP* 129). The past appears in a markedly material fashion, disturbing the innovation and modernity of what Boz calls "these times" (*PP* 129). The sudden visual juxtaposition of then and now undoes the present moment in one manifestation of "the intricate forms of unevenness and confusion" (Williams 1977, 129) by which the historicity of identity is made possible. The city's "historical" identity refuses to slip into a homogeneous representation; it resists accommodation within a discourse reliant on the stability of what Williams calls the fixity of an "habitual past tense" (1977, 128). We must take account of that which we see, therefore, which cannot be resolved in any representation that would do away with the traces of the other as the signs of a past that informs our identity. As *Pickwick* brings to light, the modes of perception by which an act of "historicization" takes place in nineteenth-century textuality are far from Cyclopean. They have to do frequently with *how* we see, and so see ourselves, in seeing others, in "that immanent, collective perception of any moment as a seething mix of unsettled moments" (Goodman 2004, 3), as are commonly found in *The Pickwick Papers.*

Yet despite the somewhat encrypted concern in *Pickwick* with the mechanics and poetics of vision, how we come to *see,* to *view,* that which is no longer present to us, it is perhaps a sign of its obliquity, at least with regard to the straightforwardly historical or political, that the novel *appears* not particularly engaged in its moment of production. In his biography of Dickens, Fred Kaplan offers the assertion that *Pickwick* is a "novel of personal myth, not history. . . . The historical world stands still in *Pickwick*" (1988, 82). John Bowen comments that "the book seems for the most part indifferent to politics, concerned to create a discursive space above and beyond them. . . . *Pickwick* may be the least politically or socially focused of Dickens's novels" (2000, 76). While both critics' languages imply the transcendent and mythopoetic, thereby leaving out of the picture any necessity for seeing history differently, Dominic Rainsford offers a more sympathetic response: "In *Pickwick,* Dickens does not attempt to cover up social iniquities, but he is not prepared to involve himself in them heavily" (1997, 103). Perhaps Dickens refrains from involving himself because Boz remains unable to judge, given the unreliability and undecidability of that to which he can only bear indirect witness. The novel thus posits an ethical dilemma in facing up to the past (or avoiding this, knowing that such a "face to face" is impossible).

However we might wish to read the problems of history and the political, it is perhaps a sign that something has been lost in translation between the initial transmission and reception of the novel in the 1830s and critical commentary on Dickens at the end of the twentieth century, that *Pickwick* appears to have become if not invisible then somewhat overlooked. *Pickwick*'s relation to what we may blithely refer to as its historical, material, political, and cultural contexts is not available to observation. To risk hyperbole, it is as if the rest of the nineteenth century and particular views of that century get in the way of seeing *Pickwick,* obscuring our view. In the face of this, it appears somewhat prudent—however simple or obvious this might sound—to suggest that modes of historical perception and transmission are no longer the same as they were in the first half of the nineteenth century.[10] Connecting the materiality of inscription with feeling, Christina Crosby claims that "nineteenth-century British thought is *indelibly marked by* . . . a *passion* for 'history' and faith in historical explanation of all sorts" (1991, 1; emphasis added). In observing a connection between the ineradicable inscription on epistemology and the pulse of the emotional force that drives that inscription, Crosby delineates what she terms the "epistemological and an ontological principle" of history for the Victorians as the "determining condition of all life and therefore of all knowledge" (1–2). In this illustration of nineteenth-century historical thought and the significance of such thought in all its forms for the understanding today of cultural identity, Crosby implicitly calls into question the very possibility of the "dispassionate spectator." That double emphasis on thinking and passion announces the historicity of reflection and perception irreducible to any single form, methodology, or practice. As a reflection of this apprehension, a careful reading of *Pickwick* brings to light the fact that the modes of perception by which an act of "historicization" takes place in the nineteenth century are far from Cyclopean and, once again, have to do equally with how we see ourselves *in* seeing others.

The good reader of *Pickwick* will be aware already of this matter of self-consciousness and its auto-reflexive turn. Understanding this, it must also be admitted that one cannot justifiably argue for one historicizing mode, either in the text of Dickens or as the means by which to read Dickens—even though a good deal of historicist criticism in recent decades has sought to impose such monolithic imperatives repeatedly. Often such reading has functioned through the wielding of a single keyword or families of such words, such as "power" or "sexuality," "surveillance" or "policing," the "family" or the "state." While this has been a widespread critical concern not limited to Dickens, one result of what might be called a will to historicization on the part of literary and cultural criticism in the last three decades and its production of a particular nineteenth century is that

Pickwick is now, if not invisible, then consigned to intermittent moments of revenant appearance. It is as if the buoyant excesses of the novel present an ineradicable problem for those cozy confluences of critical perspective intent on producing a world where every moment of agency or play is ultimately recuperated into an affirmation of oppressive power structures. What is missing from such critical activity, of course, is a necessary reflexive self-reading. If we were to glance slyly to one side for a moment, as *Pickwick* invites us to do so many times, and observe the historicist critic observing the Dickensian text, might we not witness a subject produced "historically" (as it were), and one who in being always already recuperated—and hence powerless, co-opted—seeks to superimpose that displaced and occluded self-vision on some other location?

A monocular, not to say myopic historicizing view of Dickens will doubtless produce a reading in which what Jeremy Tambling calls Dickens' "reactionary stance" (1995, 13), generated as it is from a complex complicity with "petit-bourgeois ideology" (215) and expressing at times a "combination of repression and calculation" (215), leads to the signs in the text of Dickens of "proto-fascist violence" (13). But such a reading, though produced from a perception that there is a discernible "lack of an adequately articulated contestatory ideology [that] marks an absence in British nineteenth-century politics" (13), arrives as a result of its own combination of repression and calculation; for this reading of Dickens, violence, and the modern state, has little to say of either *Pickwick* or *Nicholas Nickleby*, referring to the novels in passing a total of three times (12, 54). In this reading, what *is* visible in *Pickwick* is the appearance of Warren's Blacking Factory (12), where Dickens was apprenticed as a child. Subsequently, a comparison between *Pickwick* and *A Christmas Carol* drawn from Steven Marcus suggests a "lapse" into an "escapist mode" of narrative that signals a refusal of "modernity" (1965, 54). Surely, though, the refusal is on the part of the critic; and it is a refusal to see differently or, indeed, to see difference—and to acknowledge that difference is a markedly historical matter, the invisibility of which to particular critical modes offers a keener focus on the perspective of criticism than it does on the texts in question.

In the face of such critical armory *Pickwick* gives way; it vanishes to a degree, if not entirely. Where, then, does *The Pickwick Papers* appear in criticism? Its appearances take place for the most part in works by critics interested in what Tom Cohen has called a "philosophically inflected amalgam of programs interfacing linguistic concerns with the redefinition of 'history'" (1998, 5). Reading the historical, and reading in the wake of the traces it leaves behind, is often a matter of looking in two directions (at least) at once, as we have had occasion to observe; it is also a matter of learning to see those brief flashes of which Walter Benjamin speaks. Again it has to be said that particular modes of critical evaluation that determine themselves as "historicist" appear unable to see this or to see along these lines. Distrusting feeling, perhaps *passion* even as one sign of historical engagement or intervention, they impose their own monocular blinkeredness or myopia on the texts of Dickens (as well as other authors) without necessary awareness or respect for that other that signs itself in that indelible mark in nineteenth-century thought. This is nothing new, however, and not simply a symptom of recent criticism with a historicist or politicized focus. Take, for example, two brief commentaries: one offered by Catherine Gallagher and, at a quite different historical moment, with a markedly different ideological purpose, another by George Eliot. Gallagher, following Eliot's assessment of Dickens, suggests that the author of *Pickwick, Bleak House,* and *Hard Times* "correctly reproduces signs but misses their significance; he fails to render the network of metonymic associations connecting social conditions, character, and its external signs" (1985, 223).[11] Gallagher's commentary on Dickens' representational "failure" seems a somewhat sophisticated way of saying that he just does not join up the dots correctly. She thus superimposes the political on the aesthetic in a commentary on the limits of Dickens' historicization of his material, instead of seeing that the aesthetic may articulate the political, the historical, and material in another fashion. Part of the problem here is that signs appear to be read as if they were more or less simple or faithful representations belonging to the production of a larger representation, rather than arriving themselves in some encrypted form. There is an almost invisible sleight of hand worked by Gallagher, in her occlusion of the difference of the aesthetic through a seemingly formalist semiotic rhetoric as the key to a "properly" historical register.

Gallagher's perception of representational breakdown does not admit to the possibility of a novel operating through "a fictional economy," as John Bowen has it. Such an economy may have as much, if not more, to do with a certain figurative or emblematic articulation as it does with representation of the contemporary social world. Dickens' figurative economy, apropos *Pickwick,* is one of "impulse, excess, and misdirection" (Bowen 2000, 79) and one in which the "interest in radical social change" shared with its "Romantic precursors" is figured "through the use of what are essentially pastoral conventions" (77). Apprehending this, it should be clear that Dickens is inviting us to *feel* as well as to *see.* Dickens structures the possibility of perception and phenomenological vision through an anachronistic modality that allows access to a vision via formal revenance. The other speaks and one is caused to tremble (whether with laughter or by being "moved," being "touched") by the power of that spectral return. However, the blind spot in Gallagher's assumption prevents her apprehension of such a mode as being *properly historical.* For Gallagher, following or co-opting Eliot, in order to be *properly* historical (and therefore *political*), there can be *only one register,* and that is the one shaped by a stringent mimetic fidelity to how things are supposedly. The very idea of such fidelity echoes the notion of the imposed stability of form and representation criticized by Raymond Williams. But what, precisely, *does* George Eliot see? What is it in Eliot's essay that is the key to reading Dickens for Gallagher? For Eliot, Dickens' writing is limited inasmuch as it encourages "the miserable fallacy that high morality and refined sentiment can grow out of harsh social relations, ignorance and want" (1963, 272). The essay by Eliot just cited is also the one to which Gallagher refers, "The Natural History of German Life: Riehl," published in 1856, when *Little Dorrit*—Dickens' savage political satire of governmental failures during the time of the Crimean War—was also being published serially. Although there is not the space here to go into any great detail about Eliot's essay, what can be said so as to shed light on the sympathetic resonances between her reading and Gallagher's is that Eliot assumes that art has a duty not to falsify what she calls, somewhat monolithically, "the life of the People" (271). That capital P presumably operates as some kind of code for the working classes. It therefore effectively aestheticizes and blinds us to heterogeneity and difference. In this discussion, not only is "falsification" (271) condemned on the grounds that the artist's duty is "sacred" but such misrepresentation is read as a "perversion" (271) because the writer does not show in an objective and detached fashion the "actual" conditions of so-called existence.

Is Eliot correct? Is there a "perversion" in the Dickensian mode of representation, in the way in which Dickens *sees* and asks his readers to bear witness? Or is it not that Dickens reads signs and the network of their relations differently, and that he reads, *sees,* difference in that network and the signs the network generates? Is it not the case that Dickens, like Wordsworth before him, understands history, the past, and indeed contemporary social conditions that produce the "life of the People," as examples of what Alan Liu calls "evacuated ontology," so that collectively they inform *Pickwick* with an "absence that is the very possibility of the 'here and now'" (1989, 39)? Christina Crosby argues in her reading of *Little Dorrit,* "sentiment is Dickens's *forte,* and he uses it to manage history as effectively as Eliot uses speculative philosophy. . . . melodrama provides Dickens with a mode that is 'historical' in its insistence on a past that is lost but not forgotten" (1991, 70). Dickens wagers everything on the past not being forgotten through the structuring forces of sentiment and melodrama. That absence that is the very possibility of the "here and now" becomes visible through the effects of anamnesis. If *Little Dorrit* "represents the social in profoundly nostalgic terms, creating a melodramatic, mythological system in which 'history' is a matter of loss and gain, of absence and presence," whereby melodrama and sentiment serve actively to construct and construe "'society and history'" in order to consolidate "the middle class, its identity and its values" as Crosby avers (96), then *The Pickwick Papers* is readable in part as operating somewhat similarly.

Importantly, Crosby's commentary acknowledges implicitly the possibility of reading the work of mourning and anamnesis as signs of a certain otherness emerging not in opposition to, but instead from within sentiment and melodrama as alternative historical modes. If Dickens' historicizing "system" is a matter of "loss and gain, of absence and presence," these are not static binary oppositions, but, as we shall come to see, the former appears from within and exceeds the latter. It becomes the work of writing—and, along with this, editing, reading, and the transmission and translation of narratives, in general, through a relay or network of texts and voices—to bear witness, to bear the responsibility and burden of that manifestation of history named memory. Understanding this, it is arguable therefore that *Pickwick,* unlike *Little Dorrit,* which is very much a domestic melodrama and thus concerned with the reconstitution of the home as Crosby demonstrates, does not "consolidate," or it does not do this solely. Rather, in creating a world close enough to be remembered by its readers, a world apparently present only a decade before (but what a decade!), and yet readable as rapidly disappearing, vanishing from sight as "the ever receding ground of the present" (Crosby 1991, 96), *Pickwick* projects the very possibility of nineteenth-century middle-class national identity as a condition of loss, absence, and undecidability. It does so in two principal ways: first, through its close attention to matters of vision and sight, and the often comic consequences that arise as a result of the unreliability of interpretation stemming from empirical evidence; and second, through its relentless proliferation and circulation of texts (letters, found tales, and manuscripts), various forms of communication, and the multiplication of embedded stories within the principal narrative. Dickens, like Scott before him, responds to a "demand for an approach to the past that would interest a middle-class public by treating aspects of experience with which they could empathize . . . in a manner that would engage their imaginations and their sympathies, thus allowing them, as it were, to experience the past anew" (Rigney 2001, 71) through that solicitation of the subject by the force of sentiment.

In beginning to bring this chapter to a conclusion we should say a word or two more about sentiment, a term and concept so often associated with Dickens (and to which we will return in the final chapter). His contemporary, Anthony Trollope, referred in one of his novels to Dickens as "Mr Popular Sentiment," as is well known. Equally familiar is Oscar Wilde's assessment of Dickensian sentimentality, in a throwaway aside allegedly made to Ada Leverson. Though Wilde himself never wrote it down, he is supposed to have remarked, in response to the ending of *The Old Curiosity Shop* (1840–41): "One must have a heart of stone to read the death of Little Nell without laughing." Dismissals such as these have continued to resonate down to the recent past in criticism. When Kevis Goodman remarks of Romantic new historicism that "the significance of some kind of 'feeling' . . . as a mode of historical manifestation is an underexplored or undeveloped *insight*" (2004, 4; emphasis added), she offers a comment appropriate to the reading of Dickens from particular historicist perspectives. More than merely mawkish feeling that fails to make the right connections or otherwise perverts representation, sentiment can be a powerful, conservative tool, as the quotation from Christina Crosby above shows. Sentiment is not, however, simply an emotional distortion, even though too much of it can cause this. Following Crosby, Adela Pinch, and Kevis Goodman,[12] it must be stressed that sentiment is not the sign of an individual or central subject. It is, to cite Goodman, a figure of affect denoting a "corona of forces and effects extending inward and outward from the body" (2004, 145 n. 12), which is most directly perceived in *Pickwick* through the structural relay of vision. Of course it should be remembered that sentiment can cloud our vision. It can make us misty-eyed. What we think we see swims before us, and thus it is all the more necessary that we find a means of focusing that is clear-sighted.

On the other hand, we must not forget that sentiment does not always signify the misrepresentation of an excessively emotional perspective, thought, or view; indeed, as we shall see through the example of Rachel Wardle's view of Tracy Tupman, sentiment is available, in *The Pickwick Papers* at least, to a cynical and satirical consideration. Not taken too far, sentiment, the *OED* tells us, is an awareness gained from vague sensation, a mental feeling; it is the feeling or meaning intended by a particular passage, its intent no doubt being to "affect the eye of the beholder," as Brook

Taylor has it in my first epigraph; or it is a wish or view expressed as an epigraph. What all these definitions share is an apprehension of the subject's phenomenological translation. When not taken to extremes, sentiment is, or can be, in some of its eighteenth- and nineteenth-century manifestations, another name for the structural play of perception and conscious experience. Put another way, sentiment figures simultaneously both the inescapability of perceptive interpretation and the risk of a certain misapprehension arising from the very same consciousness. Sentiment doubles itself in a contradictory, not to say paradoxical or even perhaps an aporetic fashion. Inseparable from itself into two distinct conceptual formations, the notion of sentiment oscillates undecidably. How do we decide whether sentiment offers the proper perspective or an overly colored view? There are at least two ways to look at sentiment, and the very idea of sentiment is inextricably caught up in the question of how one sees, as well as the processes of translation that are always intimately entwined in the act of looking.

The last thing we need, therefore, in order to read *The Pickwick Papers* is some pseudo-scientific lens, which prosthetic device is reliant on the ideological illusion that its view is mimetically and therefore historically accurate. As Raymond Williams emphasized in an interview, "there is no natural seeing and therefore there cannot be a direct and unmediated contact with reality" (1981, 167). A monocular view of the novel and its relationship to history is not only unhelpful; it is disingenuous, not to say, once again, myopic or blinkered. The Cyclopean or monocular is to be distrusted especially in the text of Dickens, as the character of the sadistic schoolteacher from *The Life and Adventures of Nicholas Nickleby,* Mr Wackford Squeers, gives us to understand, his monstrousness being captured in the following physiognomic detail: "He had but one eye and the popular prejudice runs in favour of two" (Dickens 1986, 90).

This is not merely a somewhat felicitous quotation serving to illustrate my point metaphorically and wittily (though it is to be hoped it is this also). For, as with our previous illustrations of Quixote-Pickwick and the doubling of the editor and the editor effect, there is also an historical echo in this commentary on villainy, Dickens having adapted the observation from a line of Richard Brinsley Sheridan's *The Rivals* (1775; III.i). While the lines in Sheridan's play are merely a comical remark on the part of Captain Absolute concerning his preference in the matter of women's features, Dickens' comic device is historically specific. The Yorkshire schoolmaster's idiosyncratic physiognomy has a rhetorical and ideological purpose—a fiercely satirical polemic exposing the abuses of a number of schools in Yorkshire, established from the mid-eighteenth century, for the purpose of obscuring from everyday sight illegitimate and other "unwanted" children, for those families who chose to send them to such institutions. A visible synecdoche, to do with what one chooses to see and, as the phrase has it "turning a blind eye," the single eye serves as a figure for all that is wrong with Squeers and, by extension, both his school and a political culture that allows such schools to exist. The feature makes possible a moral indictment, thereby opening the readers' eyes to otherwise occluded contemporary social practices. As Dickens' historicization *and* estrangement of the quotation through the grotesque comic register of the commentary indicates, we require a technology of looking and reading that can focus in different directions simultaneously, which is capable of bringing into view certain otherwise overlooked idiosyncrasies of detail; and which will "produce something other than a singular history, which will tell us something other than the story of the same" (Crosby 1991, 108). Charles Dickens' first novel offers us just such an optical system, in a narrative where, it must not be forgotten, comedy and play have as much force as sentiment.

2

Vision's Difference

"Yes, I have a pair of eyes," replied Sam, "and that's just it. If they wos a pair o' patent double million magnifyin' gas microscopes of hextra power, p'raps I might be able to see through a flight o' stairs and a deal door; but bein' only eyes, you see, my wision's limited."
—Chapter 33, *The Pickwick Papers*

With the first vision, the first contact, the first pleasure, there is initiation, that is, not the positing of a content, but the opening of a dimension that can never again be closed, the establishment of a level in terms of which every other experience will henceforth be situated. The idea is this level, this dimension.
—Maurice Merleau-Ponty, *The Visible and the Invisible* (1968)

I. Seeing Nothing

At the beginning of chapter 25, we witness the following scene, in which an idea is bodied forth:

> . . . the mob, who, indignant at being excluded, and *anxious to see* what followed, relieved their feelings by kicking at the gate and ringing the bell, for an hour or two afterwards. In this amusement they all took part by turns, except three or four fortunate individuals, who having discovered a grating in the gate which commanded *a view of nothing,* were *staring* through it, with the same indefatigable perseverance with which people

> will flatten their noses against the front windows of a chemist's shop, when a drunken man, who has been run over by a dog-cart in the street, is undergoing a *surgical inspection* in the back-parlour. (*PP* 328; emphasis added)

As David Trotter has so perspicaciously—and perspicuously—observed, "the microscopic inspection . . . seems to require as its complement a macroscopic inspection, which . . . produces nothing at all" (1996, 215). Yet again, a double scene: of looking and looking at nothing; of nothing to see, and the analogy that structures the passage between one moment of collective observation and another. Or perhaps we might suggest that the latter observation on the collective gaze projects the phantasmic, analogical image of the former. Such duplication and reduplication stages four distinct locations from which the look is directed, each involving an observing narrator and observed crowd.

And yet the supplementary scene is not *of* the order of narrative events; the nearly silent shift to present tense—people will flatten their noses against the front windows of a chemist's shop—introduces that which Raymond Williams defines in a discussion of Dickensian narrative form as the "hypothesis of a perspective" (1983, 161). Looking, if not exactly fruitless, in response to the paucity or absence of any referent turns back on itself. The very idea that motivates the act unveils itself as far from pointless. It is that which is *in* the vision, which we come to perceive. In the face of seeing nothing empirically, we come to see "the invisible *of* this world . . . its own and interior possibility" (Merleau-Ponty 1968, 151). Let us look closely at the structure of the scene, its order and its content.

The observers, observing nothing and yet intent on "staring," are themselves transformed into the "something" to be looked at; they become the vision and the source of a commentary on the collective gaze. Their act of looking makes them worthy of extended, hypothetical observation. Through the refraction of the relay that structures focalization, the reader is illuminated about the comic nature of the collective gaze through editorial reflection, in which the invisible scene—those people with their flattened noses—and its own microscopic double—the surgical inspection and the image of the imagined man undergoing such inspection—appears as the iterable double, the phantasmic other, of its visible counterpart, the anxious mob. Another vision is suggested in this moment, a strange uncanny projection. The violent anterior scene of a drunken man being run over by a dog-cart hovers for the reader as yet one more imagined *a priori* event. There is a disordering temporality within and *as* the very possibility of this structure. Any distinctions between that which is internal or external to the narrative are erased by the multiplying lines of sight even as the distinction between the empirical, albeit mediated vision and its phantasmic counterpart crumbles. To state the order of form as straightforwardly as possible: structurally, response to the empirical scene is followed, in the face of nothing, with the magnification of the primary scene's idea, itself given projected form; the supplement takes on a greater force than the prior moment as, in being *invented* from within the inaugural instant, it passes from the invisible to the visible. The dimension of vision is opened from within itself, the idea of vision assuming a more coercive currency than any mere representation of some supposed empirical referent.

That anxiety to see that informs the mob's persistent view of nothing arises as the perhaps disquieting manifestation of some collective scopophilic desire. It might be said that the editorial intervention in the moment and its reflection leading to the ghostly arrival of that abyssally structured analogy with its temporal regression invites the reader to see oneself. For reading, it can be argued, is precisely just this "looking-at-nothing" in the desire to conjure a vision. In Dickens' structural and visual hyperbole—my own analytical hyperbole being merely itself an indirect reflection and not necessarily a magnified distortion of Boz's overstatement—we perceive that the author "adds . . . a register that turns the story itself into an object of representation" (Grossman 1997, 188). And, we would add, a narrative about, on the one hand, the re-presentation of representation while, on the other hand, a representation of re-presentation. We find ourselves involved in a world of endlessly shifting perspectives, in which frequently Mr Pickwick, setting out as a *spectator,* one armed with spectacles and telescope for the aid of bringing detail nearer and into focus, repeatedly "becomes himself a spectacle" (Miller 1958, 16).

The very act of looking constitutes a provisional identity, but it is an identity always in ruins in which the glance or gaze is implicated. In this volatile slippage where no character, subject, group, or event can ever hope to remain stable upon being viewed, we find charted the contours and flows of what Raymond Williams describes as nothing less than the visualization of that which is materially "lived and felt" (1977, 132). We perceive what Williams calls one of those "structures of feeling [that] can be defined as social experiences in *solution*" (1977, 133). Boz's revelation of the shared structures of perception and the visual as that which opens to our gaze the non-synonymous structures of feeling accord a mobility to narrative that refuses to acquiesce to any fixity of representation.

Furthermore, it makes possible the presentation of a "*perspective* which is [otherwise] not socially or politically available" (Williams 1983, 161). In this it renders *Pickwick*'s vision as other to its times and irreducible, either to any simple or simply determined past or to any simply assigned ideological location or frame. Having entered what Merleau-Ponty terms the "strange domain" of vision's ideality, "one does not *see* how there could be any question of leaving it" (Merleau-Ponty 1968, 152; first emphasis added). *Pickwick*'s vision acknowledges this everywhere, and on each occasion that it stages this inauguration, this opening onto, and invention of the world of vision. In doing so, it makes visible "a force [Dickens] knows not to be in the existing balance of forces that was there [in the 1830s] to be observed" and so *in-forms* what Raymond Williams gropes to find a language for but settles on describing as "a crucial variable in the question of realist fiction" (Williams 1983, 161).

II. The Visual Matrix

One of the most visible details of *The Posthumous Papers of the Pickwick Club* is the insistent, iterable, recurrence of motifs, figures, and terms having to do with visuality, vision, observation (in the multiple sense of sight, intellectual consideration, and critical commentary), the visible, and visible effects.[1] There is sight. There is seeing, there being around 600 conjugations of the verb and of course the act it names in the novel. Eyes are everywhere, nearly 500 of them (or, if these are pairs, then around 1,000); people are observed observing (206 times), and reflecting on their observations (64 times), while others observe the appearance of eyes; there are spectacles (67 in all, and of two kinds, those that are worn and those that take place as public events). Appearance itself has a noticeable frequency; it appears in various forms more than 330 times. Though scarce, references to optics are to be found, as is one mention of magnification. Apparitions have their moments, though they only appear indirectly, being the ghosts belonging to tales told by various characters, whose stories are interpolated/interpellated[2] into the principal narrative of Samuel Pickwick and his companions. We witness visions, and there are occasional devices such as telescopes and microscopes (whether literal or metaphorical) for aiding vision and for making visible that which is too far away to be seen with the naked eye.

All such figures are presented, apprehended, or intimated to draw attention to *how* one perceives and the ways in which one fails to see how one does not necessarily see—or read—correctly. They are gathered in order to show the necessity of looking carefully, even if they are not to be governed in the act of reading, as the examples of the mob at the gate and the crowd at the chemist's window shows us. Though taking place "outside" the narrative, reading translates the visible marks on the page into visions for the mind's eye, visions that come to be "inside" us, occupying our imaginations.[3] Such transference is presented and performed in the example with which we began this chapter. As Susan Horton has noted, "in the Dickens world, this kind of play with visuality is not unusual . . . Dickens' narration regularly turns readers into watchers of characters watching one another watching, often watching one another's reflections" (1995, 1–2).[4] This very odd, not to say uncanny, structure—which, it should be noted, is also a form of transport—is of course remarked upon by Dickens, albeit indirectly, in those highly entertaining but interruptive narratives, such as "The Sexton's Tale" or "The Bagman's Story." The vignettes push their way into the foreground, interrupting the movement of Mr Pickwick's narrative, and demanding that we look at them. They appear directly to the reader, the double mediation of the respective tale's narrator and Boz becoming transparent, if not invisible, in the process. Finally, it has to be admitted that if one can see, and if there are things to see, whether real or imagined, literal or figural, and if secrets "come to light," as the phrase has it, there must be some manifestation or source of light or illumination, of which there are nearly five hundred examples in the novel.

As the figures of observation and sight suggest, tropes of vision also comment on processes of thought. For example, one frequently says "I see," meaning "I understand." There is thus a motion, if not a slippage, at work in the language of vision as well as in vision itself in *Pickwick.* That words such as "spectacle/s," observation, and sight operate in *The Pickwick Papers* in a doubling manner, whether directly or implicitly, indicates an instability in language to which I have just referred. More precisely, there is acknowledged that which takes place between the material mark of the word on the page and that act of seeing involving interpretation that we call reading. It is as if the verbal signs signifying vision are themselves haunted; or, at least their structures are not internally coherent. They appear to threaten to unloose themselves from the page. Of course, such linguistic disturbance and flux—or, as I have already had occasion to refer to it, *translation*—is there from the start, located as it is in the various titles of Dickens' novel. For, while it is most commonly referred to—and printed as—*The Pickwick Papers,* it is also titled *The Posthumous Papers of the*

Pickwick Club; and furthermore, as we saw in the last chapter, it is also, once again, *The Posthumous Papers of the Pickwick Club containing a faithful record of the perambulations, perils, travels, adventures and Sporting Transactions of the corresponding members.* However, the various rewritings are not what concern us here. Nor are we directly interested in the aporetic encounter with undecidability that is designated through the multiplication and instability of titles. For, as just announced, there is also that fluctuation to be seen in single words and phrases. In solution as it were, such words allude more or less indirectly through the process of flux and transport to a fraught relationship between seeing and reading, between vision and textuality, between the empirical, historical event and the inscribed record.

To put this differently, something is at work between the very idea of narrative *qua* representation of a history and the material act of writing as envisioning, whereby memory is made visible. The immaterial is given a quasi-material support. There occurs what Jean-Luc Marion has called an "invisible transpiercing," by which the reader witnesses "a world sometimes more visible than the real world" (2004, 11). Something takes place in Dickens' writing between the verbal and the visual, the unseen and the seen. Strictly speaking, however, this "something" is nothing as such, neither material nor "real." Far from offering the closure of any meaning, identity, object, or event in place through modes of representation, that which takes place causes representation to admit of a disruption emerging from within itself and in the very act of representation's coming into being. It is as if, in the very mark on the page there is a disturbance in the field of vision, which disruption, though invisible, is always already under way. It is as if these non-synonymous figures relating to vision are haunted by, or disclose themselves as, examples of phantom syllepsis or zeugma waiting expectantly to be completed. Now Dickens employs zeugma on a number of occasions in *Pickwick* with telling comic effect (*PP* 69, 353, 369, 482, 662, 720). Consider, for example, either "all the girls were in tears and white muslin" (369) or "he threw off his green spectacles and his gravity" (662). The tropological immanence of such destabilizing rhetorical movement in the language of vision is more than merely comic, even though on several instances or at various narrative junctures it is this. As with all such doubling figures we do not know quite how *or* where to look, as it were. In either case, each of the statements making up the pair could be verified with our own eyes, were we able to see. But we are not. The potential play between literal and figural signals a certain material register embedded in language simultaneously in plain sight and yet also, for all that, secretive, encrypted. The noticeable incidence of such figures and their tropic dimension is all the more intriguing because the frequency of their appearance seems to bear no direct relationship to the narrative, other than to draw our attention to acts of seeing and, often, their precarious conditions.

Acknowledgment of a few examples should suffice to indicate the apparent oddity of the recurrence of those terms that make up this constellation of the visible. In chapter 2, Mr Pickwick's spectacles are knocked off (a frequent occurrence throughout the book) during a dispute with a cabman (*PP* 22). In the same chapter, he applies "a telescope to his eye" to view the "'fine old castle'" at Rochester (*PP* 28). In this particular moment we do not see directly what the telescope reveals, obviously enough. However, Jingle's ruinous telegraphic speech enacts indirectly the "magnificent ruin," as it is apostrophised by Augustus Snodgrass: "'glorious pile—frowning walls—tottering arches—dark nooks—crumbling staircases . . . earthy smell . . . little Saxon doors . . . queer customers those monks'" (*PP* 29). Jingle's language is at once a fragmented vision of the scene and its past; taking, we might say, the long view, it may also be read as an encrypted delineation of or telescopic insight into the necessary elements of Gothic architecture and the Gothic novel. The invisible scene of the past returns within the depiction, itself displaced from the magnified image presumably present to Mr Pickwick's eye.

Following the meeting with Jingle in this chapter, in which a tale is told and an appointment for dinner is made, Mr Pickwick, consulting his watch, remarks, "'let me see.'" Clearly, the remark refers both to the act of looking at the timepiece and reflective consideration. In response to the Jingle's tales of poetry writing and dog-keeping, Mr Snodgrass and Mr Winkle remark in turn, "'I should like to see his poem'" and "'I should like to see that dog'" (*PP* 29), both men expressing mild desire to have before them the empirical correlates of the phantasms conjured by Jingle's narrative. In chapter 8, there occurs a curious instance when Mr Tupman and Joe, the fat boy as he is often called, consider one another at length (*PP* 110). The passage is peppered with figures of vision. Mr Tupman "looked around," in response to Joe's "large circular eyes," which were "staring." That the eyes and not the fat boy are staring is somewhat unnerving, uncanny perhaps, but explainable partially because Joe apparently suffers from some form of narcolepsy. Mr Tupman, in return, "gazed at the fat boy," and reciprocally, "the fat boy stared at him." Once more, Mr Tupman "observed" Joe. A potentially infinite relay of gazes is established, leading to no definite information, meaning, or knowledge; for Mr

Tupman convinces himself that "he either did not know, or did not understand, anything that had been going forward." Of Joe's appearance we are reliably informed that "the most expert physiognomist" could not have deciphered the fat boy's lack of expression. Sight, seeing, and visible appearance are intimately connected to the impossibility of certain interpretation. The economy of editorial process gives way before the aneconomic opening of the gaze.

There are many other such moments. "The Bagman's Story" begins with a conditional clause involving the possibility of observation that seems to invoke preternaturally the opening of a novel by Thomas Hardy—"'One winter's evening, about five o'clock, just as it began to grow dusk, a man in a gig *might have been seen* urging his tired horse along the road, which leads across Marlborough Downs, in the direction of Bristol'" (*PP* 185; emphasis added). What follows, though, is anything but Hardyesque; this being a *Pickwick* narrator, he self-reflexively draws attention to the moment of the view within the narrative structure: "'I say he might have been seen, and I have no doubt he would have been, if anybody but a blind man had happened to pass that way; but the weather was so bad, and the night so cold and wet, that nothing was out but the water . . .'" In the gesture of presenting to his audience's hypothetical view the limited visibility due to the time of day and the atmospheric conditions, the narrator recalls the Boz of the *Sketches* who makes the paradoxical claim that "the streets of London, to be beheld in the very height of their glory, should be seen on a dark, dull, murky winter's night . . ." (Dickens 1994, 55). This comparison aside, though, in its inauguration through the vision—in both senses—of a phantom subject, "The Bagman's Story" operates through another of those hypotheses of perspective addressed by Raymond Williams.

On another occasion in chapter 14 (*PP* 266–67), Sam Weller's father appears for the first time in the novel and to the reader through a series of repeated looks, stares, gazes, and observations directed toward Sam and Mr Pickwick. In the course of two paragraphs, the first of which begins with an apparently straightforward "description" of a room in an inn, our attention is drawn to a "stout man" who has also "attracted Mr Pickwick's attention." We thus have our attention directed to two different locations, the second of which involves our seeing Mr Pickwick looking at Tony Weller; from this moment of doubling and division, we are treated to a virtual visual semaphore: "looked," "another look," "look," "stare," "see," "Mr Weller's observation," "he saw Mr Pickwick's eyes every now and then turning towards him," and "he began to gaze." Such insistent and frequent glances are not limited to any one character. In chapter 22, in which Mr Pickwick travels to Ipswich, Mr Peter Magnus examines Mr Pickwick for "several minutes" through his "coloured spectacles" (*PP* 297). Mr Magnus also requires, and at length receives, what Boz describes hyperbolically as "ocular demonstration" (*PP* 294) that his baggage has not been forgotten.

Later in the same chapter, having left his watch on a table, Mr Pickwick goes in search of it, peeping into "room after room." Becoming lost in his search of the Great White Horse Inn, his eyes are "astonished" at the apparently labyrinthine structure of the stairs, which uncannily just seem to "appear" (*PP* 299). Having found his watch, he then proceeds to try to locate his room, which he believes he has found by peeping in once again (*PP* 300). This is not his room, however, as he discovers once he is in bed when someone else enters the room. From this point, Mr Pickwick "catch[es] a glimpse of his mysterious visiter [*sic*] without the least danger of being seen himself . . . by . . . peeping out from between the [bed] curtains" (*PP* 301). We are then informed that "nothing more of him could be seen than his face and night-cap, and putting on his spectacles, he . . . looked out" (*PP* 301). Before him, and before a "dressing glass" (one of many optical instruments in the book) stands a "middle-aged lady" who, despite filling Mr Pickwick with dread, causes in him "the urgent desire to see what was going forward" (*PP* 301). Peeping out a third time, Mr Pickwick observes the lady "gazing pensively on the fire" (*PP* 303). This wholly voyeuristic moment comes to an end when, in a moment of Gothic parody, Mr Pickwick exposes himself—a "sudden apparition" in a night-cap. Here we witness another of those disabling suspensions of narrative where the gaze is structured as a reciprocal relay, potentially endless in its form: "she stood, staring wildly at Mr Pickwick, while Mr Pickwick in his turn, stared wildly at her" (*PP* 303). The parody of the male stalker-voyeur given form in Mr Pickwick's Peeping Tom is rendered in that moment when Pickwick, appearing as the ghost of himself, has his gaze returned, both characters seeing in the other the distorted reflection of their own fears. As in the scene between Tupman and the fat boy, the reciprocal circuit of the gaze offers to open abyssally in its immanent infinitude, while causing narrative motion to idle. Here, however, Dickens doubles the effect performatively, for he not only structures the scene as stare returns stare, but with a slightly off-kilter quasi-symmetry structures the sentence iterably through the phrase "staring wildly" and its return as "stared wildly."

The Posthumous Papers of the Pickwick Club is peppered with such illustrative cases. Not only are stares, looks, gazes, observations, and "meaningful" looks marked (*PP* 312); there is also that proliferation of eyes mentioned. Sam "eyes" Job, while Job's eyes fill with tears, and he applies a pink handkerchief to his eyes (*PP* 311, 312). Tom, the protagonist of "The Bagman's Story," is noted for "marking . . . little evidences with the eye of an experienced traveller" (*PP* 187). This eye wanders, however, on the occasion of Tom becoming sentimental (*PP* 188). He comments also on a "smartly dressed girl" as having a "bright eye" (*PP* 187). The "principal figure in Mr Winkle's visions" is "a young lady with black eyes" (*PP* 368). Mr Pickwick's lawyer, Mr Perker, suggests the strategy of throwing dust in the judge's eyes (*PP* 410), which, however obviously metaphorical, nevertheless conflates comprehension with vision. On his way to Leadenhall Market, Sam's journey is repeatedly interrupted. Passage through the city and passage in the narrative are both called to a halt by vision because, as we see, Sam pauses occasionally, he loiters in order to "contemplate" and to "gaze" (*PP* 431), his eyes eventually caught by a particular representation. In searching the stationer's window, Sam's eyes are "fixed" by the sight of the Valentine's Day card (*PP* 431). The operation of the eye is obviously inimical to motion, whether it is a matter of travel or reading. And of course, there is Sam's telling and highly astute rejoinder to Sergeant Buzfuz, in the case of Bardell v. Pickwick, concerning the power and limits of eyes, as opposed to that of the "patent double million gas microscope" (of "hextra power" [*PP* 464]), which is cited as the epigraph to this chapter. As Sam makes transparent, eyes can no more see through the architecture of a building than they can see into the past without some artifice, some prosthetic device for the production of the visible from the invisible, whether that apparatus be the microscope, as in Sam's illustration of the problem, or the editorial pen, as we go on to discuss.

We must not pause too long, however, having idled already in observing and reflecting on only a few instances. To move more rapidly, there are to be observed "horn spectacles" (*PP* 594), a "gold eye glass" (*PP* 473), "green spectacles" (*PP* 508), yet more spectacles (*PP* 629, 637, 639), and "a clerk in spectacles" (*PP* 540). In addition, we see "brilliant eyes" (*PP* 477). At the Ball in the Assembly Rooms, Bath, in another of those social spectacles, certain ladies, including the Dowager Lady Snuphanuph, "no sooner set eyes upon Mr Pickwick" than "they exchanged glances" (*PP* 480). Mrs Dowler shrieks as a result of having "caught sight" of events in the street, while, in the same scene, "the first object that met the gaze of both" Mr Dowler and Mr Pickwick is Mr Winkle (*PP* 493). Having fled Bath for Bristol, Mr Winkle walked "forth to view the city" and soon "his eye fell upon a newly painted tenement" (*PP* 506). On instructions from

Mr Pickwick to follow Mr Winkle, Sam was, we are told, "determined not to take his eyes off him" (*PP* 519). Spying on the lodging of Miss Arabella Allen, Sam is "concealed from view," while "his eyes [are] fixed upon the dust heap" (*PP* 522). Additionally, we are told, "shaking little pieces of carpet" is "not half as innocent a thing as it looks" (*PP* 524).

Chapter 41 opens onto a scene of Mr Pickwick opening his eyes, while Sam engages in "a comprehensive gaze"; Mr Smangle attempts the fruitless activity of "staring" Sam "out of countenance," which is of no avail, of course, because Sam, ever indefatigable, continues "to look steadily" at Smangle (*PP* 557). Mr Pickwick acknowledges the relationship between seeing, understanding, and interpretation, when he says to Sam, "I see you comprehend me" (*PP* 570), which idiom is structured by its abyssal play between *see* and *comprehend.* (Pickwick's remark could as easily be written, "I comprehend you see what I mean.") In a more encoded moment, there is "a perfect alphabet of winks" (*PP* 576). More philosophically, there is also a "Platonic wink"—whatever that might be—directed toward a young lady (*PP* 595). Mr Pickwick gazes in astonishment (*PP* 592), while "Mr Stiggins . . . turned up his eyes" (*PP* 599). The Bagman, who makes another appearance in the novel (every apparition is always double, at least implicitly so), is described by Sam as the "gentleman with one eye" and that eye, we read, is "intently fixed" on the landlord of the inn. Upon seeing Mr Pickwick, the Bagman remarks, "'I've seen you before . . . '" (*PP* 642). Solomon Pell's eyes "glistened" as a sign of his legal interest (*PP* 729), while Samuel Pickwick's eyes "moistened" in the company of his friends (*PP* 749). And finally, at the close of *The Pickwick Papers*—or almost finally, for there is a supplementary coda, following the conclusion—the so-called "editor" (*PP* 15) of *The Pickwick Papers* claims to have no "optical powers" for seeing the darker aspects of human existence, and so encourages us to join him in taking "our last parting *look* at the *visionary* companions . . . when the brief sunshine of the world is blazing full upon them" (*PP* 752; emphasis added). This last remark announces forcefully a commerce between the visible and invisible, the power of a form of transport or translation in which a certain kind of sight is involved, and which, moreover, is made possible through the agency of the letter. Everyone is gathered in the individuated community, a community without unity, of the look.

Doubtless each of these illustrations is worthy of further, more considered analysis. A last pair must suffice, though, before we move on to the next part of the chapter, both coming from Mr Pickwick's residence in the Fleet Prison, a place of many sights and spectacles (*PP* 547). In looking for accommodation for Mr Pickwick on his arrival at the Fleet, Mr Weller replies to a comment of Mr Roker's concerning the quality of a prison room by the "closing of one eye," the meaning of which encrypted ocular telegraphy is undecidable (*PP* 546): "Mr Weller replied with an easy and unstudied closing of one eye; which might be considered to mean, either that he would have thought it, or that he would not have thought it, or that he had never thought anything at all about it, just as *the observer's imagination* suggested" (546; emphasis added). The comedy of the scene only works if the reader knows ahead of Boz's comments what Sam means and so sees it "in a flash," as it were. On the strength of Boz's inability to say anything other than to say that he cannot say and that meaning resides in the imagination of the observer and whatever might come to the mind's eye, the reader is faced with the aporetic experience, however amusing an instance of the undecidable this might be. Again, Boz's envisioned observer has appeared, as if to announce that we are in the ghostly presence of yet another hypothetical perspective. Boz provides the optical aid in the form of the phantom observer and his or her phantasmic imagination, but resolutely avoids showing how to make a decision in the face of a complete absence of evidence. No description or representation of the room shown Sam by Mr Roker is offered. There is nothing to gather about the condition of the accommodation from Mr Roker's rhetorical question, "'You wouldn't think to find such a room as this, in the Farringdon Hotel, would you?'" (*PP* 546). In short, we see nothing. There is nothing to glimpse other than that "unstudied closing of one eye." Thus, however slight the example, and however disproportionate the explanation—mine or Boz's—the reader is put in a position of having to *see,* to *imagine,* without the evidence to weigh, and so to comprehend through a crisis in representation that which only sight can convey, however faulty or mediated. At the limit of writing, only imagination's vision can attest.

A similar event of bearing witness is staged for the reader. While in the prison, Mr Pickwick has occasion to "peep" into various rooms, thereby allowing the reader to see various inmates, who are only "just visible" (*PP* 546). The hypothesis of perspective arises once more:

> In [an] adjoining room, some solitary tenant *might be seen,* poring, by the light of a feeble tallow candle, over a bundle of soiled and tattered papers, yellow with dust and dropping to pieces from age, writing, for the hundredth time, some lengthened statement of his grievances, for the perusal of some great man whose eyes it would never reach, or whose heart it would never touch. (*PP* 546–47; emphasis added)

Immediately before this, Mr Pickwick has witnessed some prisoners smoking and drinking beer. Following the passage just cited, a number of other prisoners are seen. But from his comment to Sam—"'It strikes me, Sam, that imprisonment for debt is scarcely any punishment at all'" (*PP* 547)—it is not clear that Mr Pickwick *does* see the scene quoted; if he does, he does not see that to which Boz provides witness and envisions—the invisible within the visible, the narrative that gives us to see the reason for the prisoner's incarceration. Again, vision exceeds the empirical facts. A double presentation is offered—of solitary reading in which, if it is not too fanciful, the reader is invited to see oneself. More than this, though, the reader can glimpse the past that informs the present, and beyond any immediate or recent context, the traces of other past moments, to which the yellow, tattered papers silently yet graphically attest. The visionary force is all the more powerful for the risk it takes in seeing the invisible, and so reading inventively through the inauguration of a fiction the structure of feeling. In being asked to see, we are also asked to feel, to see ourselves simultaneously as the solitary tenant *and* someone whose eyes *do* "peruse" both a statement of "grievances" (Boz's representations of incarceration) and the visualization of suffering through such sentences. In the doubling that takes place between the verbal and visual image through the mediation of what *might be seen* a perspective on society *in solution* is opened, which, to recall the words of Raymond Williams, is otherwise not socially or politically available.

III. Diminishing Difference

The frequency of so many figures of vision and sight and their tropological operation is fascinating. But on first glance it is also, perhaps, somewhat perplexing, as I have had occasion to remark. The very frequency remarked through so many graphic instances causing the narrative to stutter might be taken as a curious manifestation of some spectroscopic wavelength. Why this repetitive occurrence takes place in *The Pickwick Papers* cannot be answered absolutely. One might propose cautiously, however, that the proliferation of the tropes of visuality and vision in Dickens' text is readable as a symptom of broader epistemological and ontological changes in the nineteenth century. We can address such changes briefly. A sense of a doubled, and therefore a divided, subjectivity comes to be produced in the early part of the century specifically in relation to sight and the optical. For Rosalind Krauss, the effect is one of phenomenological uncanniness, brought about by the dissolution of psychic boundaries caused by technological advances. Optical devices such as the zoetrope put the viewer simultaneously outside and inside the experience of watching. As she describes what amounts to a doubling simultaneity, "I'm *in* this experience; I'm *watching* this experience" (Krauss 1988, 58). This disturbing duplication of subject position is arguably analogous with that phantasmic experience of the reader, already described. This experience of a troubled subjectivity is echoed elsewhere. As Susan Horton comments in the wake of Jonathan Crary's work on techniques of observation, the Victorians "were caught between two models of vision: that of the empirical senses, which were proving the eye of the observer unreliable and subjective [and therefore in principle open to the translations and editorial effects of sentiment], and that of the various romanticisms and early modernism, which posited the observer as an active, autonomous producer of his or her own visual experience" (1995, 8).

The historicity of the subject-position as informed by visual experience would appear, in Dickens' first novel at least, to be *in solution* (to call up Williams' phrase once more) in such a manner that resonates with the perceptions of optical-subjective phenomena as proposed by Krauss, Horton, and Crary. Though not a study of optical devices and the psychic effects of visual technologies, the present volume notes the sustained disturbance to the subject in *Pickwick* in just such terms. The effects described above are clearly visible, even though the commanding technology of the visual is not an optical device but the editorial pen. In apprehending the fluidity perceived and mediated by Boz we may, in turn, catch sight of a far less static condition of subjectivity than that for which words such as "caught" or "model" allow. As we see in *The Pickwick Papers,* whenever certain observers believe themselves to be "autonomous producers," misreading, instability, and disruption all take place. At the same time the eye of any given character as observer is notoriously unreliable, and the image it produces and relays equally so. Moreover, such is the dissolution of boundaries affected by particular performative effects in Boz's writing—as we shall have occasion to consider in the rest of the present chapter—that the reader encounters the disquieting experience of both *watching* and being *in* the experience. If Boz does not situate his characters or readers as caught, exactly, he at least places them *in suspension,* and so in a medium within a vignette of the event, in which there is subjective and visual flux—between locations, between perceptions, between sensations or emotions, and occasionally between the present of the event and the memory or image of another temporal moment.

With this in mind, we will consider in some detail three scenes, from chapters 2, 7, and 38, which mobilize figures of vision in the service of narrative effect. The first two examples have to do with affection, infatuation, and desire, and all three invoke figures of sight within or touched by a quasi- or pseudo-scientific resonance.

Our initial illustration is briefly described. At the charity ball in chapter 2, on seeing the stranger make advances to the widow, Dr Slammer ("of the 97th") cannot "believe his eyes." So shocking is the *spectacle* that "He looked again, and was under the painful necessity of admitting the veracity of his optics" (*PP* 36). There is a marked reiteration here, which is also a duplication and an amplification, concerned with belief and sight. The term "optics" intimates a scientific discourse in a manner that "eyes" does not. However, with this last example a second look is rather like a second opinion. In addition, it leads to an intensification of focus and a concomitant intensification of description resulting in comic hyperbole occasioned by the renewed examination of the empirical evidence. In the course of observation, the passage produces a performative effect from within, and in excess of the initial constative observation.[5] In its act of doubling iteration, the passage enacts, rather than merely describes the event. Having looked once and unable to trust the empirical evidence, Dr Slammer takes a second, closer look as if to confirm what his eyes tell him, despite the initial denial of his senses. The passage reproduces this structure in its rhetorical double take, and so itself supplements in a gesture of magnification the supplementary gaze that it observes. Writing performs precisely what it shows the eyes as having already done. Text thus arrives as a supplement to sight, and allows the reader to "see" in a motion analogous with that of the event to which the reader does not have access. The performative condition immerses the reader in the fluid suspension of the moment: simultaneously, I am *watching* the experience and I am *in* the experience. What I watch, what I am involved in, is not simply what Dr Slammer sees, but a doubling observation of, and implicit reflection on how Dr Slammer looks, and looks again. The image I envision concerning the act of sight and its phenomenal effects becomes my experience of that image, the experience of the structure of feeling figured by the scene, in this example a "feeling" of disbelief. In this supplementary process, the hyperbole effects a distance from the actions, which effect may arguably be read as a strange reiteration of that already doubled aporetic experience of Dr Slammer's. The "distance" effected, which is also the sign of difference, is initiated in the movement from Slammer's outraged disbelief to the reader's comic incredulity, mediated by Boz's skeptical manipulation. To borrow from Henri Lefebvre's analysis of the look, "observation and meditation follow the lines of force" that are traced in the act of looking and which flow between the differing, differentiating times and locations of sight. However, while for Lefebvre such lines are rejoined in the observer as if there were some possibility of scopic reenactment of the illusion afforded by classical perspective, for Boz they can never come together. Temporal difference and the sentimental affect of perspective inform the different times of microscopic observation and the lines of sight by which it is structured with a kind of parallelism.

Turning to our next example, in chapter 7, Isabella Wardle's infatuation with Mr Tupman is recorded in optical terms. "In her eyes," we are told, "Tracy Tupman was a youth; she viewed his years through a diminishing glass" (*PP* 96). The initial metaphor whereby emotional perception is rendered as sight orients the sentence. As in the illustration of Dr Slammer's optically inspired doubt, feeling and vision are intimately entwined. In both cases we come to see how, in the words of Jonathan Crary, "our physiological apparatus is again and again shown to be defective, inconsistent, prey to illusion, and, in a crucial manner, susceptible to external procedures of manipulation and stimulation that have the essential capacity *to produce experience for the subject*" (1990, 92). That metaphor beginning the sentence does double service. It figures at the same time both the distortion that Romantic fascination lends to the gaze as well as offering indirectly—through a kind of rhetorical refraction—a supplementary "lens" through which the reader is able to "view" what is invisible, Miss Wardle's "translation" of Tupman's physical appearance. This "translation effect" works to reveal the power to make visible, however cynically or satirically, the ways in which sight is never simply empirical observation. We "see" Miss Wardle all the more clearly because we gain insight into the way in which she views the beloved other. The translation is all the more effective because in neither part of the sentence does the metaphor fall into the weak device of simile. Mr Tupman does not "appear"; he "is" a youth to Isabella Wardle. The reader is thus directed to look in two places at once. In this opening of the structure of the image, the moments that make up the instantaneity of the gaze are restored, magnified, and so revealed in their hitherto invisible suspension. However, Boz is not content to leave it at this. It is not merely a matter of the unveiling of the work of a phenomenological, interpretative process economically registered in the figure of sight. In the second part of the sentence Miss Wardle's "sight" is aided artificially. A technological prosthesis is introduced as a medium of viewing in between subject and object when it is revealed that "she viewed his years *through a diminishing glass*" (emphasis added). We see here another performative doubling akin to that already witnessed in the language describing and observing (twice) the reiterated gaze of Slammer. The second clause is, effectively, an enlargement of the work of the first part, the sentence thereby moving in its operation from the constative to the performative.

Boz's happy choice of phrase "diminishing glass"—the term would appear to recall the earlier use of "optics"—should not be overlooked. It offers the reader a view of a slight though perhaps important cultural, historical significant trace. Though so small as to pass unseen, the term has all the interpellative/interpolative force of the various tales that interrupt and suspend *The Pickwick Papers.* A somewhat antiquated, not to say anachronistic term by the nineteenth century, "diminishing glass" was employed figurally. Amongst the first to employ the phrase was Richard Hooke (1635–1703). Hooke devised the compound microscope (the "diminishing glass"), reporting his findings in his *Micrographia* (1665), a work that not only reveals the significance of the microscope to the scientific community but also addresses questions of light and illumination,[6] and is thus one of the decisive texts in the emergence "of a modern and heterogeneous regime of vision" (Crary 1990, 3). As with the example of Dr Slammer's "optics" and the invocation in chapter 8 of a hypothetical "physiognomist," there is to be witnessed in "diminishing glass" the trace of a certain medico-scientific discourse, albeit one that is seemingly inconsequential. In light of Boz's skeptical appropriation of both phrase and, metaphorically speaking, optical technology, it is interesting to extend our detour briefly, in order to reflect however sketchily on the contested ground of the use of microscopes and the philosophical debate from the 1660s to the early nineteenth century. While in the twentieth century "[m]ost attempts to theorize vision and visuality are wedded to models that emphasize a continuous and overarching Western visual tradition" (Crary 1990, 25), the "diminishing glass," following its invention, was viewed in some quarters with suspicion. It was understood as belonging to what "Dutch physicist and instrument maker Pieter van Musschenbroek (1692–1761)" described as "'systems of imposture,'" and was regarded as being the subject of manipulation, false interpretation, and "fantastic speculation" in contrast to empirical objectivity, "'subtle analysis, [and] a scrupulous precision'" (Stafford 1994, 140, 144). The microscope or diminishing glass was all too easily subject to misuse at the hands—and eyes—of unscrupulous charlatans who sought "to deform and manipulate images and to designate as facts obscure or ambiguous occurrences"

(Stafford 1994, 144). Though it is hardly likely that Dickens was aware of the debates, the self-deceiving example of Isabella Wardle demonstrates that, a century and a half after Hooke, there was still the shameless misapplication of such technology, albeit in a figural manner. If Boz receives a somewhat encoded history of technologies of vision, however accidentally, his language also finds itself inscribed by a contested discourse on the interpretation and misuse of visual phenomena.

Yet scientific cynicism and suspicion in Europe notwithstanding, Hooke's demand for a "return to the plainness and soundness of Observations on material . . . things," which was to "begin with the Hands and Eyes, and to proceed on through the Memory . . . to come about to the Hands and Eyes again" (*Micrographia* 5, 7) was not without much appeal to the modern English mind with its empirical cast, in all its heterogeneous manifestations and discursive expressions. With this in mind, broadening the context and lengthening our detour somewhat, it is important to recall that, long before the Victorian obsession with optics, and Boz's use of the visual, the eye as trope and metaphor "with its language and models for conceiving intellectual labor" dominates eighteenth-century political economy and literature, as Kevis Goodman recalls (2004, 40). She goes on to remark, the "topos [of the "microscopic eye"] leaves its mark in the prose of physico-theological conservatives like Richard Bentley and that of early eighteenth-century rationalist philosophers like Berkeley and Locke; it informs the works of Swift and Pope; and it moves into georgic-descriptive verse by John Philips, Christopher Smart, Henry Baker, and Richard Jago, as well as" Goodman's principal example, James Thomson (40). There are furthermore "at least seventeen works specifically on the subject of perspective between 1715 and 1800" (de Bolla 1989, 186).[7] Particularly, it is Thomson's poem *The Seasons* that Goodman reads for its application of the "microscopic eye" to the English farming landscape in all its historicity, and which text serves to produce a vision of Englishness.

With its mocking adherence to, and parody of, pastoral conventions, *The Pickwick Papers* also employs, even as it distances itself from, a similar vision of Englishness, which in the distance and difference of the years between 1828 and 1837 is seen to be passing away. If, as Wordsworth claimed in 1815, Thomson taught "the art of seeing" (cit. Goodman 2004, 38), Boz teaches his readers to distrust the pedagogy of the eye, or at least to be suspicious of any claims to clarity or supposedly unmediated vision. Concomitantly, he educates his reading public to see the defects and distortions if not with a jaundiced eye then certainly more clear-sightedly. For as much as Dickens' first novel is indebted to the forms of the novel in the eighteenth century,[8] it is also the case that there is to be found at work a "spectatorial model" (Goodman 2004, 40), the genealogy of which is indebted to various discourses belonging to the period of, but not restricted by the texts of, Addison and Steele, Defoe, Fielding, and Richardson, amongst others. *Pickwick*'s references to the panoptical array of sight- and vision-related terms partakes unmistakably of and is encoded by the previous century's obsession with the gaze and its accompanying lexicography. The tropology of the eye and its non-synonymous cognates works in conjunction with satire, cynicism, and irony in order to produce what Goodman describes as a "discordant affective awareness" (40) on the part of the reader. Such awareness arguably produces an estranging disjunction that is temporal, separating the reader in all his or her modernity in the 1830s from the visible signs of the distant and recent pasts, out of which is produced *Pickwick*'s comic capital.

To ignore or downplay the function of the figures of vision is to distort the view of the past in relation to the present of the 1830s, and therefore to misread the traces that structure the narrative of *The Pickwick Papers.* Furthermore, it is to miss the signs of the novel's historical and material moment of production and, moreover, to miss taking the long view, whereby the historicity of a "moment," so called, can be seen not as an instant but as a complex perspective traced in and by the materiality of the letter. In short, one misses reading the text in all its nascent Victorianism. For, in reading the interlacing traces by which we come to see Samuel Pickwick and his friends, and to distance ourselves through affectionate laughter and cynical disbelief, we find ourselves ensnared by what Jonathan Arac calls a specifically "Victorian mode of writing . . . [which] include[s] the articulation and interweaving of particular 'cultural codes'" (1979, 123, 134).

To return to the scene with which we were concerned: via the medium of the novel's "self-consciousness about sensory mediation" (Goodman 2004, 41), it is as if we are to understand, to imagine in the mind's eye, as it were, Miss Wardle placing Tupman under a microscope. Far from "diminishing" him in her eyes as a close inspection might, the spinster's phantom prosthesis amplifies all those invisible qualities, attributes, and details that are unavailable in the unmediated image of Tracy Tupman. We comprehend that Rachel Wardle does so in order precisely *not* to see him as he is, but to "translate" him into, we might say, the ghost of Tupman past. The "diminishing glass" produces a memory of Tupman, one that cannot be Miss Wardle's. Even as this takes place, the forensic inquiry is held up in turn to the "scientific" questioning and skepticism on the part of the editor of *The Pickwick Papers* in the very process of ironic, destabilizing narration. To reiterate: Miss Wardle's sight and the language in which it is couched reveal how technological prosthesis enables translation *and* visibility. Bringing the invisible to the naked eye, it nonetheless foregrounds the unreliability of such processes. Yet, despite the cynical humor and its appeal to a rational view of the distortion that takes place here, the double question of translation and visualization with regard to how one sees or misperceives the past has broader implications for reading *Pickwick.* There might be seen an effort on the part of Boz to draw our attention to the condition of novel writing, its construction of views of the past and the historicity of its mediation of vision as, specifically, a material if not historical problem. The figures of vision, sight, and the eye encourage us to read in greater detail the act of novel writing as a self-conscious questioning of the "literary mediation of the historical field" as Kevis Goodman has it (41). Dickens is readable perhaps as raising the problem of the role of the novel in the early Victorian present, where, to paraphrase and extend a statement by Georg Lukács (1972, 157), "the problem of the present," and concomitantly the auto-perception of one's modernity available in any attempt at self-reading is inescapably apprehended as a material and "historical problem," however indirectly that may come to be *represented.* As the example of Mr Tupman illustrates, there is no such thing as an unmediated vision. We should always be wary of *how* we see; we should look at the mechanisms by which we claim to produce a vision or image.

One further illustration shows this problematic effectively, specifically in terms of scientific discourse and the role of observation. In chapter 38, there is the case of "the scientific gentleman" and his observations, which, once more, addresses the history of scientific discourse, empirical evidence, textual record, and the unreliability of narrative accounts of what one believes one has seen (*PP* 529–32). Boz's focus on the "elderly gentleman of scientific attainments" (*PP* 529) directs our gaze away from the comic assignation between Mr Winkle and Arabella, aided and abetted by Sam Weller and Mr Pickwick. This shift of attention effectively suspends the narrative movement with its own counternarrative, but this is not the only suspension. Pausing in the act of writing and "gazing abstractedly" into the night (*PP* 529), the "scientific gentleman" is observed by the narrator "observing" (*PP* 529) a series of apparently inexplicable lights, the "appearances" of which "had [n]ever been seen before" (*PP* 530). So the brief story of the scientific gentleman continues, with the words relating to sight and appearance dancing before the reader with as lively a frequency as the "unparalleled appearances" of the enigmatic lights themselves: "the scientific gentleman seized his pen again, and committed to paper . . . the date, day, hour, minute, and precise second at which they were visible. . . . The mysterious light appeared more brilliantly than before. . . . he rang the bell for his servant":

> "Pruffle," said the scientific gentleman, "there is something very extraordinary in the air to-night. Did you see that?" said the scientific gentleman, pointing out of the window as the light again became visible. (*PP* 530)

The frequency of Boz's comically irritating repetition of the phrase "scientific gentleman"—it occurs eleven times in three pages—is itself a highly visible interruption, analogous with those flashing lights. Pruffle's assertion that the lights are probably signs of burglars is met with derision on the part of the "scientific gentleman," who decides to leave his library (where he had been seated) in order to carry his research into the field, at which point the narrative returns to the misadventures of Mr Winkle and his friends.

However, the narration does return to its account of the scientific gentleman in the final paragraph of the chapter:

> As to the scientific gentleman, *he demonstrated in a masterly treatise that these wonderful lights were the effect of electricity,* and clearly proved the same by detailing how *a flash of fire danced before his eyes* when he put his head out of the gate, and how he received a shock which stunned him for a full quarter of an hour afterwards; which demonstration delighted all the Scientific Associations beyond measure, *and caused him to be considered a light of science ever afterwards.* (*PP* 331–32; emphasis added)

The obvious references to sight, vision, visibility, and observation in these few pages aside, the conclusion moves from the conceit of the visible in relation to scientific and philosophical knowledge being lampooned here to a number of matters. These concern the materiality of writing and, implicitly, its inherent untrustworthiness either as a technique for visualization or for bearing witness either to evidence or experience, in the wake of unreliable subjective perception. A doubt is raised as to the possible illumination that textuality can provide in the absence of materially verifiable visible objects or phenomena. As the passage illustrates with such economic relief (and much of that being as comic as it is graphic), the interest has to do with textual transmission and therefore writing, its translation of empirical evidence. The comic effects of showing the scientific observer as being in error shed a distanced, ironic light on the veracity of his own recordings, his written "scientific" observations. Despite the necessity of recording history so as to remember the past and bear witness to it, or providing a written record as account of the interpretation of empirical evidence, writing is far from being a reliable process; it is internally fraught. Such "translation" destabilizes rather than fixes meaning, as the singular example of the lights' undecidability becoming the source of writing for the scientific gentleman, regardless of their true "material" source, shows.

The scene begins as one of reading and writing. We witness, through Boz's mediation, a private moment of interrupted reflection and analysis on the part of the scientific gentleman, who, "seated in his library," is "writing a philosophical treatise" and is caught "in the agonies of composition" (*PP* 529). The narration concludes with the editorial recollection of the eventual production of "a masterly treatise" (*PP* 531). Yet, as we have just had occasion to observe, the acts of writing and observing are analogously, and notoriously, unreliable. A double writing is seen to take place, occurring between the seen and the unseen. One text is visible, while the other remains invisible. The former is the production of the "editor" of *The Pickwick Papers,* the latter text that of the scientific gentleman. The elderly observer might be seen (if this is not too fanciful) as an uncanny double of Mr Pickwick;[9] he might also be readable perhaps, partially, as the counterpart to Boz, as a future anterior phantasm of the currently fashionable observer of the passing world, himself become anachronistic. We witness the bifurcation and opening of all writing as medium for observation and reflection. We encounter the relay and fraying of the textual act and its modes of visualization, its illustrations and representations, where a supposedly single act of writing is seen to be haunted already within itself by that which it traces and seeks to represent. It is inescapably double in its weave between the visible and the invisible, which the two textual evidences simply make manifest through the self-conscious illumination of their presence and absence. We read one, that of *Pickwick*'s editor, and through its presence we read the absence of the scientific treatise, while also reading a(n admittedly distorted) paraphrase of that treatise, which stands in for, and thereby transmits, translates, relays that which cannot be present *as such.* A slippage takes place in writing, and this is seen as the very condition by which writing has its chance of being the material bearer of the traces of the past. In making visible that which is not present, inscription changes irrevocably, even as it mediates; every act of writing (and reading, it must be admitted) is a betrayal as well as a gesture of fidelity to the vision it desires to figure. It cannot help but be this, and Boz knows it.

He knows it and makes much of the comic, graphic potential, as the final paragraph demonstrates. For there is that movement of illumination from the literal to the metaphorical that is borne by the vehicle of writing. From seeing lights in the dark, the scientific gentleman "sees" those flashes of fire, the phenomena resulting from having been hit on the head accidentally.[10] A motion is traced from the external, empirical world and the unreliability of eyesight to the parody of enlightenment as a result of insight and mental illumination. From this occurrence, the old man is enabled to write that treatise, the result of which is his own "translation," by which he becomes transformed into "a *light* of science ever afterwards" (emphasis added). From the enigma of empirical evidence to neurological disturbance, and from this to the doubtful illumination of faulty knowledge, whereby further scientific insights are seen—and all by the fortuitous motions of writing caught up in the signs of the visual and visible. This internal, loosening play is not something that gradually comes to take place. It is there from the beginning of the scene. It is there in the library, in that place, to make the point again, where writing takes place and where it is suspended, as the scientific gentleman looks literally, and in vain, for inspiration. He looks repeatedly at the carpet, the wall, the ceiling, and out of the window (*PP* 529). *Pickwick*'s editor makes the twinned processes of suspension and observation highly visible. Subsequently, the reader comes to see the suspension, a moment in time caught reiterating itself. For we are informed about and thus invited to visualize the elderly gentleman who, in attempting to write, is caught in the act "*ever and anon* moistening his clay and his labours" (*PP* 529; emphasis added). This instance of syllepsis relies on the slipperiness that ensues from the performative operation of the verb, as at the same time the repeated application to alcohol in a "venerable-looking bottle" (*PP* 529) is sought in order to make the writing "flow," as it were. That writing cannot be turned on like a faucet is given evidence in the implications of the phrase "ever and anon." Thus writing, in its very material appearance, marks the page with an irreconcilable binocular oscillation between the visible and the invisible, and within which the possibility of movement is suspended, sight questioned, and nothing is to be taken at face value.

3

Illuminating Difference

Are we not Spirits, that are shaped into a body, into an Appearance; and that fade away again into air and Invisibility? This is no metaphor, it is a simple scientific *fact;* we start out of Nothingness, take figure, and are Apparitions . . .
—Thomas Carlyle, *Sartor Resartus* (1833–34)

"What strange things these are you tell us of, Sir," said Mr Pickwick, minutely scanning the old man's countenance, by the aid of his glasses.
—Chapter 21, *The Pickwick Papers*

One can be the "anachronistic" contemporary of a generation past or to come.
—Jacques Derrida, *Archive Fever*

I. The Modern English Subject

That prosopopoeic synecdoche for spectral legions of amateur researchers of independent means, the "elderly gentleman of scientific attainments" with whom we concluded the previous chapter, is associated with light and with illumination, in several ways. The first association has to do with literal light. As we have seen, the empirical fact of its appearance is separated from the misinterpretation that arises from it. This separation leads to a moment of epistemological enlightenment, however dubious or risible this may appear to the reader through the focus offered by Boz.

This in turn survives beyond the event to become a scientific "paper" with its own powers of illumination. There is subsequently another related though discontinuous form of illumination. Through the publication of his "masterly treatise," the anonymous scientific gentleman—whose very anonymity appears to ensure his signifying role beyond his immediate being—becomes also a beacon of light in and for the scientific community. The elderly amateur scientist's presence in the novel accidentally brings to light one dimension of the historicity of bourgeois male life across the long eighteenth and nineteenth centuries, of which Samuel Pickwick is yet another example. Mr Pickwick himself publishes treatises, to the existence of which Boz attests. One "paper" to which we are referred is Samuel Pickwick's "'*Speculations* on the Source of the Hampstead Ponds, with Some *Observations* on the Theory of Tittlebats'" (*PP* 15; emphasis added). Unfortunately, we never get to read this; it remains invisible. Another writing stands in its place, alluding to it but never citing it, and so opening from within itself a sight of one more doubling, discontinuous relay. The title, which, it is to be observed in passing, contains references to both mental reflection and empirical observation, is a satire on historical documents of the mid-eighteenth century, as Mark Wormald, editor of the Penguin Classics edition of the novel, observes in a footnote to Pickwick's title (*PP* 775 n. 1). As Wormald suggests, Dickens' titular satire recalls not only a paper presented to the Royal Society in 1747 by William Arderon but also to a paper satirizing the earlier paper, published in 1751 by John Hill in his *Review of the Works of the Royal Society*.

There is also more than this at work, though. The title of Mr Pickwick's paper serves as oblique synecdochic indication of the historical and cultural identity out of which Mr Pickwick emerges and in which historical composite he is situated. Reading anamorphically, the title places Samuel Pickwick, however wryly, ironically, or comically, as a material product of cultural history, itself the articulation of a particular national identity in all its historicity. Pickwick's title marks him as being encoded and, perhaps, *riven* by philosophical, scientific, and ideological discourses, developed from the 1660s to the early nineteenth century. Read in this fashion, Samuel Pickwick is produced and so comes to appear before us as the typical educated "modern" bourgeois English subject.[1] As Rosemarie Bodenheimer has stated, Dickens' novels "dramatize . . . the constructedness of bourgeois subjectivity," founded as they are "on a deep awareness of the instability of class identification and of identity as a process of fissure and projection" (2001, 216). What we should remember at this point is that such subjectivity has a genealogy or history, as do all constructions of identity. The writing of Samuel Pickwick and the intimation of what he writes are no exceptions to this project. What is singularly interesting about the examples of both Pickwick and *Pickwick* is the revelation of the extent to which, attending to the more obliquely visible traces, one can read the historicity of this subject. Pickwick and *Pickwick* are singular constructs of the intellectual life of the post–civil war English middle classes, from the 1660s to the 1830s. They figure the contest of voices and the contrasting images that these envision, in the invention of one particular manifestation of Englishness.

Thus, one senses through such singular comic examples the chance illumination of a discontinuous network or relay. Or say instead, writing projects, or serves to light up its subject; and in principle at least it enlightens even as it brings to light that which previously had been in the dark, invisible. It does so in such a way as to represent representation, and to invite us to look at how we see the scene. What do we see? We glimpse beyond the individual examples a way of life; with that we obtain a view of amateur interests, wherein is to be seen the articulation of one symptomatic appearance of Englishness. With this, and the (indirectly) inferred, analogous connection between Pickwick and his anonymous doppelganger—both of them "anachronistic contemporar[ies] of a generation past or to come" (Derrida 2004b, 6)[2]—there opens to the imagination's gaze the comic perspective of countless bachelor researchers, diminishing across a number of generations, communicating and miscommunicating.

It is *as if* Dickens stages an encrypted, historicized view of the national character of a peculiarly English enlightenment and its modern emergence, dating not from the Cartesian cogito but—to give it a provisional moment of inauguration and invention—from the microscopic work of Hooke. Such identity is seen as being marked by what Peter Ackroyd has termed a "novel self-consciousness" (Ackroyd 1993, 13), the signs of which are still readable in *The Pickwick Papers.* The definition, illustrating the legacy of what Ackroyd defines as a now anachronistic modernity "which has exerted a powerful force since its inception" (1993, 13),[3] might be said to run as follows: to be English is to get things wrong, often hopelessly and comically so. But it is to get things wrong in just the same way as everyone else, who is just like you—and so to communicate a differentiated heterogeneous identity through analogous forms of miscommunication. In this "dark glass" one sees oneself reflected and refracted. Thus one becomes convinced that the meaning of one's being is true and correct in a self-reading that is also a misreading, albeit one that is productive.

In *The Posthumous Papers of the Pickwick Club* "'Experience,'" to cite Ackroyd once more, "emerges as a concept of value" (1993, 16)—and it is this, amongst other signs, which signifies a certain English modernity stretching from the seventeenth to the nineteenth centuries. Yet experience in *Pickwick,* despite placing the modern male, bourgeois subject at the center of knowledge and the world, is always caught up with empirical observation and invariably leads to chaos. It leads to misunderstanding, to misdirected communications, communications that are not understood correctly or at all, and to the perpetuation and iteration of a self-conscious act of seeing oneself *that fails to see how one sees.* Through the serious play of language Boz creates this reflection on the distortions of misperception. If it is the case that "in each situation one must create an appropriate mode of exposition, to invent a law of the singular event, taking into account the addressee, imagined or desired; and at the same time to claim that this writing will determine the reader, who will learn to read (or 'to live')" (Derrida 2004b, 6), then doubtless this is what comes to be performed in *Pickwick* for the articulation and maintenance of the phantasmic survival of a particular dimension of Englishness. Life as narrative serves as an envisioned, prosopopoeic synecdoche. Articulating a cultural imperative to bear witness, it demands that we read the traces of the other within ourselves despite or perhaps because of miscommunications. In its composition from the traces of the past, life as narrative allows a recognition of similarity and difference, all the while expressing the injunction "do not forget" (to borrow a significant memorial trace from *Little Dorrit*). That distance effected through the comedy of miscommunication authorizes the reader's memories of the past in a specific form. Cultural memory is positioned inside anecdote, vignette, intertextual allusion, and reference. It assumes in its exteriorization of the memory in the text of *Pickwick* what Marc Augé describes as "a kind of autonomy, of independence in comparison to . . . present chronology." Thus writing's "distortion" of vision's already distorted images affords the reader a "smoke-screen memory that . . . removes that which is too close to give us the illusion of perspective" (Augé 2004, 19). In its comic differentiating mode of projection and re-presentation that gives the illusion of being at a remove from the fictional events of the previous decade *Pickwick* foregrounds its estranged (because distanced) life-as-narrative through "remembrance-pictures" (Augé 2004, 21). Such phantom-phatic images in their return remind us that the events for which they stand in are doubly displaced in the processes of re-representation. From the unseen posthumous papers through the semivisible editorial intervention, writing is always materially there to produce the illusion of perspective. If Mr Pickwick or, for that matter, the elderly gentleman appears naïve or somewhat childlike, as is often suggested by critics, then this is deliberate. They are not simply childlike and thus vehicles for moral education that experience of the world affords. They figure the childhood memories, if you will, of a particular vision of Englishness, their projection onto the page bringing about a kind of annexation of the (reader's) present from the past. The memories of the past given face in *Pickwick*'s characters and providing histories in the images of their adventures recall to the reader "vanished landscapes or faces" that "haunt the common aspect of our experience" (Augé 2004, 21). *The Pickwick Papers* thus affects us through the return of involuntary memory of a culture in passing as illuminated through the life of a single character, in this case Samuel Pickwick, as he passes through countless *spectacles* of the cultural life, the cultural being, of the nation.

The novel is a virtual catalogue, a phantasmagoria or perhaps more precisely, given the date of its invention, a zoetrope ("wheel of life") of such spectacles, of elections, soirees, garden parties, military displays. Invented by William Horner in 1834, the zoetrope was an improvement on the phenakistoscope of Plateau. While the earlier invention required a mirror and thus was limited to the use of one viewer at a time, the zoetrope admitted of several viewers simultaneously and, therefore, multiple perspectives. Its cylindrical drum used constant motion to create the illusion of motion. Whether or not Dickens was familiar with the zoetrope, the combination of motion and simultaneously distinct perspectival locations in the machine's representation of life's "circular" motions is certainly suggestive as a figure for the numerous circuits and journeys of *Pickwick,* with the narrative procession of spectacles. Read with a view to the persistence of the visual, like the zoetrope *Pickwick* is, in the words of Jonathan Crary, caught up in "a much larger and denser organization of knowledge and the observing subject" (1988, 30–31). Stepping down from his chair in the Pickwick Club (quite literally as we shall see in the next section of this chapter), and thereby removing himself from a *tableau vivant* in order to take part, as it were, in the "wheel of life," Samuel Pickwick affords the reader various views of Englishness in spectacular motion. Although there is not the space to discuss these at any length, a brief overview can be offered. We see balls and soirees (*PP* 20–46, 494–505). There are representations of the medical profession, journalism, the arts (*PP* 197–210), nonconformist gatherings (*PP* 429–44), the courts, and the legal profession (*PP* 402–17, 445–67); the reader is taken inside and given a sustained view of the Fleet debtor's prison (*PP* 544–611). We witness political life and the processes of gerrymandering, as represented by Dickens' satire of the Eatanswill by-election (*PP* 165–81). An "old-fashioned Card Party" (*PP* 80–93) is depicted, as is a duel (*PP* 20–46), cricket matches (*PP* 93–106), hunting (*PP* 93–106, 245–58), weddings, and Christmas gatherings (*PP* 360–380). With a little temporal give and take, it is arguable that the scenes could belong to any moment in a seventy- or eighty-year span, from the 1740s (at least) to the 1820s. We come to see, to feel even, an odd untimeliness to the representation of such occasions. However, in presenting to the reader's view such a series of cultural spectacles from the perspective of Mr Pickwick and his friends, Boz allows the reader a "regained impression" of Englishness and thus a "return to oneself" (Augé 2004, 68). Such a return is double, of course: it takes place for the reader and Boz. This regained impression, as Augé has it, endures through an auto-identification that is staged by the text and is what *Pickwick* makes possible in its opening to a past that is not merely representational but also intertextual. For the indirect allusions to and memories of other texts are also the traces of the revenance of the regained impression that causes *Pickwick* and thus the reader to identify themselves with their pasts, but with the necessity of remarking difference from that past.

Writing is thus a tele-technology, of vision and memory. A prosthesis and substrate, it is a mnemotechnic device that mediates the self in particular ways. A singular writing of identity thus takes place, where the vision that is projected through synecdoche and analogical relay allows access to the experience of the other. This phrase, "experience of the other," operates as a double genitive, echoing with the doubled sense of visionary experience described by Rosalind Krauss with regard to technologies of vision in the nineteenth century, and cited in the previous chapter. As we read we come to *see* one figure of the other, and so to share in his experiences—hence the regained impression of a certain similarity culturally speaking. But we also come to see through our experience of the other the difference as well as the similarity. The comic confusions of the elderly gentleman translated into his masterly treatise are akin epistemologically, albeit with a difference, to Samuel Pickwick's in their "scientific" purpose of observation, misperception, and subsequent dissemination. "Boz" also shares in the misperception, though with a degree of ironic distancing, aware as he is that all empirical observation and its subsequent transmission is indelibly marked by the anachrony of the trace. His writing makes much capital from a recognition of the clinamen inherent in perception as misperception and its subsequent textual translation. The revenance of the anachronic trace affords and, indeed, makes inevitable the torque within representation that divides and doubles the image's reception so as to expose the temporal dimension, the historicity of any particular moment of being. As we have seen and continue to see, Boz's writing is reliant in the attention it draws to what we might call the clinamen of the gaze; this manifests itself in a writing, the structure of which "grafts, without confusion . . . the poetic on the philosophical." Boz has, moreover, "certain ways of using homonyms, of the undecidable, tricks of language [such as paradox or zeugma]—that many read in confusion, while ignoring the properly logical necessity for it" (Derrida 2004a, 6). And the logical necessity driving such play is the desire that the reader will see—and will see, more to the point, how the rhetoric of seeing illuminates itself in such a way as to shed light on the difference between supposedly distinct temporal moments or scenes in the historicity of Englishness. The "properly logical necessity" aims to instruct the reader in the art of seeing if not historically, then at least with an insight into the productive distortions afforded by an awareness of the difference between moments of being. The question of how one sees illuminates how one fails to see, and how one's gaze is always prey to an inclination or bias that arrives not from the experience of the viewed object or image, but from within oneself as the sign of that anachronic other.

II. In Which Chapter 1 Returns

Writing's strangeness is thus indelibly connected to the acts of seeing or making visible. More than this we may make two propositions, however counterintuitive they may seem. First: writing *is* light. Second: seeing *is* a writing also. We grasp these dual apothegms in light of the illuminating trace of the scientific gentleman, which in turn finds a kindred source of illumination mentioned in—and as part of—the first sentence of *The Pickwick Papers:* "The first ray of light which illumines the gloom . . . would appear to be derived from a perusal of the following entry in the Transactions of the Pickwick Club . . ." (*PP* 15; the first sentence will return in its entirety shortly). In the process of considering figures of vision and sight, as well as their illuminating nature, I have had occasion to allude to "scientific" and "philosophical" texts, such as are signified through the title of a paper of Mr Pickwick's, which appears, interwoven with the figure of light, on the first page of the novel. Once again, it can be seen that writing represents illumination. But it also re-presents it; it serves as a means to "cast a light" figuratively speaking on that which we cannot otherwise see. Writing thus performs as well as commenting upon the processes of illumination *and* enlightenment. In doubling itself it acts as a form of projection that causes to appear, and so come into some form of ghostly being, the magic lantern show that is literature, as was suggested earlier in a different context. At the same time in a reciprocally enfolded relation the trope of light serves to shed light on the act of writing taking place, and from there to the scene that inscription both reveals and enacts. The "discontinuities of lived duration" are momentarily and repeatedly overleapt through an evocation and invention of a "feeling of continuity" (Augé 2004, 71, 73). As I averred at the end of the previous chapter and as is implied insistently in the previous section of the present chapter, the letter and vision are closely intertwined.

This is illustrated exhaustively and excessively in the first chapter of *The Posthumous Papers of the Pickwick Club,* to which we will now turn. While considering other particular aspects of this chapter, let us extend further our consideration of the obsession with sight, its operation in the novel, and the matter of writing. In this chapter, after the first couple of pages in which we get the report of a debate drawn from various textual sources, the reader is introduced to the image, rather than the myth already implicated in the opening paragraph, of Mr Pickwick as he climbs upon his chair at a meeting of the Pickwick Club. This moment is described as a *tableau vivant,* an "exciting scene" that presents itself as a study to the imaginary gaze of a hypothetical artist (*PP* 17). Along with those other disinterested observers, the artist is one more fleeting phantom. The artist not only observes, but his or her "appearance" sheds that light by which the reader can see and is instructed to see. As with the opening paragraph of the novel, we find ourselves confronted by a lengthy sentence played out in successive clauses, which is worth quoting in full:

> What a study for an artist did that exciting scene present! The eloquent Pickwick, with one hand gracefully concealed behind his coat tails, and the other waving in air to assist his glowing declamation; his elevated position revealing those tights and gaiters, which, had they clothed an ordinary man, might have passed without observation, but which, when Pickwick clothed them—if we may use the expression—inspired involuntary awe and respect; surrounded by the men who had volunteered to share the perils of his travels, and who were destined to participate in the glories of his discoveries. (*PP* 17)

A doubled scene of writing, the textual moment is not only a representation of Pickwick; it is also a graphic delineation of the first illustration in the novel, drawn by Robert Seymour. Something quite odd takes place here, of which we would do well to take note. As we know, the passage reinscribes a history of events gathered apparently from other documents not available directly to the reader, through the work of someone who identifies himself as "the editor of these papers" (*PP* 15). Boz enacts a relay of communication from document to document that displaces and defers the visible "scene" that is being presented. At the same time the written scene arrives as a disruptive supplement to Seymour's illustration, in the double sense of being an addition *and* replacement. One form of graphic representation stands in for another, the written text acknowledging through its editorial self-reflexivity that which the illustration obscures—that there is no direct access to a past moment, or unmediated vision of that. The reader will observe an incommensurability between representational modes, where writing, as faithful witness to details and architectonic ordering of the illustration betrays its assumption of unity. Insinuating the limits of the visual representation, "Boz," the editor effect, remarks that which is invisibly under way of the deferral and differentiation that haunts, even as it makes possible, the illusory homogeneity of the illustration. Not only is the gap between verbal and visual image revealed as a matter of spatial textual relations and the difference of forms. We apprehend also a temporal tension, between absence and presence, past and present, writing and illustration, between the spacing of graphic mediation and apparent visual immediacy. The written passage illuminates the "being suspended" of the moment that is inescapable in any re-presentation or vision.

That which I have just described is generally the work of the first chapter and by extension that which takes place throughout the novel, as the story of the scientific gentleman has demonstrated. But what is immediately, unavoidably noticeable about the introduction of the "exciting scene" in which Mr Pickwick in mock-heroic fashion ascends his chair—thereby putting it to improper use, its identity as a chair being interrupted[4]—is the way in which the narratorial voice interrupts itself in order to present to our vision in one long sentence the image of Mr Pickwick. Up to this point most of the proceedings have been relayed through the reported speech of various members of the Pickwick Club, the editorial process selecting and distilling the moment from an unidentified number of written sources. The only other passage belonging to the narration "proper" is the chapter's inaugural paragraph, notable for a number of features (of which more in a moment), not least its rhetorical hyperbole tending toward the occlusion of its own matter. The interruption with which we are concerned for the moment makes possible the manifestation of the visible. Its deliberate stalling of narrative motion brings the scene to our sight. Having interrupted his own presentation, Boz focuses ever more carefully on the material details of Mr Pickwick's appearance in a temporal unfolding that is only ever immanent in the instantaneous presentation of the visual in an illustration. One kind of editing, that which is informed by diegetic drive or plot propulsion, gives way to another kind necessary for the production of character, personality, and identity, by metonymy and synecdoche, in which every visible detail serves singly and collectively to suggest the being and meaning of Mr Pickwick. Boz's sentence dismembers Mr Pickwick, only to reassemble him. Having shown us *how* to see the illustration, the editor has effectively dismantled it in such a way that we can no longer see it as a unity, but must always be aware that the act of writing the visual demands that we look, yet again, at how we see.

This demystifying illumination of the structures of focalization is already under way when our attention is first directed toward "the bald head, and circular spectacles" of "Samuel Pickwick, Esq., G.C., M.P.C." (*PP* 16). Until the observation of these synecdochic shapes, Mr Pickwick has only been figured for the reader in the "editorial" phrase (taken from the first paragraph) "the immortal Pickwick" (*PP* 15) and the subsequently reiterated proper name "Samuel Pickwick, Esq., G.C., M.P.C.," which appears five times in the first two pages (*PP* 15–16) like some stuttering act of semaphore, Morse code, or telegraphy. Arguably, the figure "immortal Pickwick" tells us little or nothing, while the synecdoche of head and spectacles articulates a double transport—significant throughout the eighteenth century in aesthetic and scientific discourses concerning perspective, the work of art, and the subject's gaze, as Peter de Bolla reminds us. On the one hand our gaze travels between "imagination and representation." On the other, the passage is "between the activities of invention and execution" (de Bolla 1989, 190). To make the point as plain as day, we are also witness to, even as we experience a transport, a translation, from the invisible and the visible. Prior to this, however, the hieratic "immortal Pickwick," a projection of the pen without clue to the signified reality or object, appears on the page, fully visible and yet undecipherable. Writing uncannily precedes and anticipates the event it calls forth supposedly after the event it claims to narrate. Imagining that we have never read *Pickwick,* when we read this phrase we see nothing: nothing concerning the identity, meaning, or ontology of a *Pickwick* other than its immortality. Writing doesn't give up the ghost; it doesn't give the game away. Certainly the novel's titles—*The Pickwick Papers, The Posthumous Papers of the Pickwick Club*—offer little to the imagination, save the idea of the existence of manuscript documents. The titles announce that Pickwick is a pronoun belonging to a club and that this is a collected, presumably ordered representation of multiple, heterogeneous acts of writing gathered together under the aegis of the proper name, or rather two: "Pickwick" and "Boz."

Nothing appears before us, therefore, even though the phrase is patently *there* in plain sight. All we can decipher is that a quality of a Pickwick is to be immortal, and immortality, as an otherwise empty and meaningless concept, is definable in the singular example of a Pickwick (whatever that is). When we do read the proper name, "Samuel Pickwick, Esq., G.C., M.P.C.," little more is unveiled without the intervention of the editor on the first page. Boz provides the helpful notes concerning the deciphering of the initials "G.C., M.P.C.," which sigla signify "General Chairman—Member Pickwick Club" (*PP* 15). Before this explanation, though, the iterability of the proper name and its encrypted appendages do nothing to suggest that they signify some extratextual referent. The referent is effectively suspended. In the frequency of iteration what becomes comprehensible is the power of writing to transport meaning and simultaneously withhold it. Writing transmits but what it transmits is its own vehicular properties, its ability to open up and take part in a relay, the operation of which is potentially endless, infinite in its deferral of meaning and independent of any presence, such as that of the supposed author of the inscription or the person to whom the proper name belongs. Repeating and rereading "Samuel Pickwick, Esq., G.C., M.P.C." over and over will get you no closer to whoever that person may be. It certainly gives away nothing, or precious little at least, about the figure, imaginary or real, conventionally assumed to stand behind that name. The proper name shows us nothing other than what Peggy Kamuf has called "the excessive mark of fiction" that disables the reader's presuppositions concerning signs and what is seen in them. If the proper name as mark only has its "'being' by virtue of an act of reading" (Kamuf 2005, 141), whatever is seen is hardly anything at all, although everything that is to be seen is there in full view.

This might seem to be giving a somewhat disproportionate degree of attention to writing, the proper name, and graphic marks generally, but then the novel itself concentrates to an alarming degree on writing, inscription, graphic marks, and related matters of iterability, communication, transport, and figurality. A slight detour is necessitated here. Often the appearances of pieces of writing insinuate themselves in *Pickwick*'s interest in the epistemology of the visual. As John Bowen has commented, "*Pickwick* is a text peculiarly concerned with language . . . it is striking how much it is the *written* nature of language that is emphasized" (2000, 51).[5] He continues: "key scenes in the book centre on writing and its absurd and uncontrollable consequences." At the same time, "if the very fact of writing and speech causes problems, so too does their transmission. The novel is very interested in the apparatus by which acts and exchanges of writing take place" (51). Although we cannot go into much detail about the effects of writing here, one need only consider briefly the following example in order to apprehend how writing and the visual are enfolded within one another. In chapter 11 we see "the following fragment of an inscription [on a stone, which] was clearly to be deciphered" (*PP* 148):

+
B I L S T
U M
P S H I
S. M.
A R K

Boz's representation of the writing as it appears on the stone has the effect of appearing to withdraw any editorial intervention or other textual mediation. The illusion is created that the reader sees the stone and its marks at the same time as Mr Pickwick, whose eyes, we are told, "sparkled with delight" (*PP* 148). A ruin from the past arrives directly before us, apparently. That it is *of* the past is re-enforced through Boz's indirect report of Mr Pickwick's knowledge of the location and its history. The county in which this is found is "known to abound in remains of the early ages," while in the particular village to which the stone belongs "there still existed some memorials of the olden time." The stone itself is of "unquestionable antiquity" and had "wholly escaped the *observation* of the many learned men who had preceded" Pickwick (*PP* 148; emphasis added). Once more, we see how specious reasoning on the part of Mr Pickwick leads to an erroneous perception that is described specifically in the relationship between writing, reading, and vision. Such is the desire to find signs of the past that they are *seen* without reflection or circumspection, while what is there—the proper name and signature of Bill Stumps—remains unseen, unread. In drawing attention to its powers to show and to occlude already witnessed at work with another proper name, "Samuel Pickwick, Esq., G.C., M.P.C.," writing once again presents itself to view as the otherwise invisible material substrate by which we see what can otherwise or no longer be seen. How we see the marks on the stone distinguishes our distance from—or proximity to—Samuel Pickwick. So we are invited to see ourselves and to reflect on our ability to see clearly.

But to return to the first chapter and the bald head and circular spectacles, these being first intimations of the figure who stands both on a chair and behind the shibboleth "Samuel Pickwick, Esq., G.C., M.P.C." The head and spectacles not only offer the reader defined, precise images; they also approximate and figure one another visually, with their intimation of partial or complete circularity in their binocular pair of curves. The head, within which is the invisible "gigantic brain" (*PP* 16), is expressed by the glasses and the glasses by the head. This analogy is borne out, given a more complex articulation in the following parallelism: "the gigantic brain of Pickwick was working beneath that forehead, and . . . the beaming eyes of Pickwick were twinkling behind those glasses" (*PP* 16). Here are the first, if not the principal visual elements in the identity of Samuel Pickwick. The spectacles and eyes come into play repeatedly throughout the novel, even if the "gigantic brain" does not as efficaciously or perspicaciously as it might. But then here is something to observe, perhaps; for if Pickwick's eyes require focusing, so too does his thinking. Assuming we are paying enough attention to visual details and reading them for what they signal beyond their immediate mimetic value, sight, the visual, the event, the spectacle: all require framing and focus, as Boz's choice of Pickwick's features lets us see. In short, they require both material support and translation.

Narrative thus interrupts itself to present to our view a related series of visual details. Mr Pickwick's "tights and gaiters" are revealed. On any other man, we are told, they "might have passed without observation" (*PP* 17). Here once again Boz's observation is doubled. The initial sight of the anachronistic dress has its negative correlative, from which it is to be inferred that our gaze is directed and focused all the more intently on the subject. From this, our sight is directed to another part of the body. One hand is "concealed," but the other waves in the air. Mr Pickwick's gold watch-chain disappears "inch by inch . . . from within the range of Tupman's vision" beneath Pickwick's black silk waistcoat (*PP* 17). There is a constant motion between what is visible and what is not in this presentation of the imaginary artist's case study, another of those hypothetical perspectives. It will be observed, moreover, that visualization is not merely the effect of editorial commentary, for attention is drawn to Tupman's "vision," to its "range." Once more we are witness to, as we experience, the ways in which the gaze is directed and issues from multiple locations while lines of sight abound, therefore confounding the notion or possibility of any single perspective. To consider briefly the role of the editor apropos perspective: one may of course read the editor as a focal point, not as a person but, as I have indicated, as an "editor effect." This involves making visible and sharpening the focus on event, character, and narrative progression in a particular order for the reader, in one order rather than another, chosen from a potentially infinite number. This occurs in any narrative, of course.

While we might understand the editor effect as an act of economizing on endless hypothetical perspectives, such an economy, however, still relies on a number of perspectives, so that the point of view from which one might see shifts and so destabilizes the monocular and implicitly tyrannical—and all the more tyrannical because invisible and silent—single perspective. Boz supports and maintains the destabilization by asserting repeatedly a lack of knowledge on a subject or the inability to determine the facts: "we have no official statement of the facts" (*PP* 20); "we cannot distinctly affirm" (*PP* 103); "we can only guess" (*PP* 144); "we cannot state the precise nature" (*PP* 220); "we cannot distinctly say" (*PP* 433); "nor can we precisely say" (*PP* 522). Note the constant deployment of the plural pronoun; "we" may be read as a sign of an impersonal, concerted structural function, an indicator of mass production, hence my earlier hypothesis of an "editorial machine." At the same time, "we" can be read as a phatic signal of sentiment: it gathers together the readers of the text, aligns them under the aegis of the titular editor. Then in its pronouncement it demands slyly that we agree with that aspect of sentiment defined by the *OED* as the sum of feelings on a particular subject. Of course the paradox is that the sentiment expressed again and again is that we can offer no definitive sentiment, much less a factual observation on whatever the subject happens to be. The *view* "we" may or may not have is obscured. The feeling or meaning remains undecidable.

The irony of every commentary that invokes "we" does nothing to help get us past the undecidability—and so our experience of the vision of the past is an experience of the aporetic. Moreover, "we," that is, the imaginary community of editor and reader produced by this particular editor effect, has no possibility of asserting anything about the past with certainty, because what was visible and once present no longer is, hence *posthumous.* This, we might say, is the truth of Boz. *We* just is the signal of a relay in a network of iterable signs that are gathered so as to offer a provisional and tentative perspective, admitting in this that there is no *one* perspective, no true vision that the narrative can proffer. Thus visualization takes place as an effect of writing in the absence of presence, certainty, or the certifiability of meaning. In apprehending the fraught condition of visualization and its multiple perspectives, we find ourselves in process. The illumination of being shows it to be *in solution* (to recall that phrase), in processes of "ideation, imagining, and remembering" (Steedman 2002, 67). As we read and therefore *watch* the experience of presentation to another, in the illustration given the vision of Mr Pickwick presented both to the reader and Mr Tupman, we find ourselves *in the experience.* We see the gaiters. We see the spectacles. In this experience representation partakes of an archiving on the part of the editor of "heterogeneous, undifferentiated stuff" (glasses, gaiters, the pocket watch are only governable within the ontology and taxonomy of a "Pickwick") that is gathered and ordered "by the principles of unification and classification" (Steedman 2002, 68). However, this is not an archivable image that will remain. Mr Pickwick will step down from his chair, out of the frame.

This is still not to be done with sight and observation in the first chapter. As has been remarked, the gaze does not issue from one place, nor is there any simple act of seeing. Someone has to "see" Mr Pickwick's twinkling eyes behind his spectacles. And no one can see everything; as is observed, Tracy Tupman's range of vision takes in part, but not all, of Samuel Pickwick's watch-chain. With regard to that bald head and circular spectacles, the following is remarked: "A casual *observer,* adds the secretary, to whose notes we are indebted for the following account—a casual *observer* might possibly have remarked nothing extraordinary in the bald head, the circular spectacles." Yet "the *sight* was indeed an interesting one;" and again: "how much more interesting did the *spectacle* become" (*PP* 16; emphasis added) when the bald head and spectacles mounted its chair in order to reveal to seemingly unobstructed view for the delight of the imagined artist (and for us also) Samuel Pickwick, of the head, glasses, and abbreviated suffixes to his title. Here the very idea of looking, albeit hypothetically, suspends the debate, and is reported as seeing not very much. It should be noted, though, that the figure of the phantom observer arrives in an indirect manner. For we are given to understand that this shadowy figure is the invention of the secretary of the Pickwick Club, and is recorded in his notes, without which the editor of *The Posthumous Papers of the Pickwick Club* could not produce in detail the "exciting scene." This is the nature of the apparition, though. It can appear and disappear as it wishes. It can travel from one place to another, from Boz's writing to that of the secretary. As we are given to see in this motion, its phantasmic illumination sheds light both on the scene and on how one comes to see that scene.

It might be objected that observation precedes any recording act that sight takes place to be followed by memory and inscription, as the illustration of the elderly scientific gentleman and his illuminating lights demonstrates. In the example with which we are presently concerned, however, Boz inverts that order. In doing so he dismantles, or at least tampers with, the framework, if not of history, then of temporal order through the structure of envisioning akin to memory. Writing arrives as editorial intervention in the guise of the careful collation "from letters and other MS authorities" (*PP* 20) in order to make visible, to illuminate. This has been stated already, but we see the inversion taking place quite nakedly in the very first sentence—which is also the first paragraph, a fragment of which we have already quoted—of the novel:

> The first ray of *light* which *illumines* the gloom, and converts into a *dazzling brilliancy* that obscurity in which the earlier history of the public career of the immortal Pickwick *would appear to be* involved, is *derived* from the perusal of the following entry in the Transactions of the Pickwick Club, which the editor of these papers feels the highest pleasure in laying before his readers, as a proof of the careful attention, indefatigable assiduity, and nice discrimination, with which *his search among the multifarious documents* confided to him has been conducted. (*PP* 15; emphasis added)

To say the least, this is a complex paragraph. Its effects and devices are many and interwoven in a labyrinthine manner. Observe primarily how the "first ray of light," while occupying the principal place in the sentence, is not as inaugural as it initially appears. For it is the case in this complex sentence-paragraph that this "first ray of light which illumines the gloom" is in fact supplementary. Derivative, secondary, its genesis is the effect of perusal, an odd word meaning both to go through, to revise, and to use up, to exhaust, to read or, as we may suggest, rewrite exhaustively (and, if this first sentence is anything to go by, exhaustingly). Light, illumination, comes as a result of reading and rereading, on which a rewriting in the form of editorial collation sheds a new light. There is something humorously reflexive and performative in the gestures of this inaugural intervention in previous texts, which is also an invention that finds in those earlier texts precisely the material that arrives from them to intervene in the editorial process. The beginning is a *rebeginning,* a return to the past through which return the traces of earlier texts. The first sentence is a revision effectively, a translation of other papers, those "MS authorities" announced at the end of the chapter, along with those "multifarious documents." The illumination provided by the "careful attention, indefatigable assiduity, and nice discrimination" on the part of "the editor of these papers" causes to make appear the scene of the opening chapter, and from there everything else in the novel. Light and illumination are thus connected to the act of making visible.

Yet what is it we see, if anything? What is converted, precisely, into a dazzling brilliancy? And far from shedding light on anything, may not a dazzling brilliancy actually blind or at least cause to obscure the very thing or event that it is intended to illuminate? All that is revealed or lighted up is the dazzling brilliancy of the complex weave of a writing that foregrounds itself. The materiality of inscription is drawn to the reader's attention through the metaphors of enlightenment that hide or encrypt knowledge in the reflective illumination of the line's own "mazy motion." We "see," if we see anything at all, a pen playing across a page, a responsive prosthesis of an otherwise invisible observer—the "editor of these pages"—engaged in the act of reading that is itself a response, as we have stated. We find ourselves in a location belonging to a relay in which there is no *first* position at all, but which intermediary condition is figured implicitly in the generation of the scene of writing from those papers, documents, and manuscripts, all of them being other scenes of writing, of course.

I spoke earlier of an editor effect or editor machine, and it would be well to recall, at this juncture, that *edit* is derived, so to speak, from Latin, meaning to come out of or give out, according to the *OED*. What comes forth or comes out is the line itself, writing illuminating its own motion, its own manifestation. Thus, in a singularly performative manner the editor effect is to make appear something out of nothing, to make visible on the page a line that sheds light on itself. And this is performative inasmuch as nothing is merely described or observed in this sentence-paragraph. The very thing being described is also executed. The illumination *takes place*. What do we see, therefore? We see writing under way, we see appear before us the illumination of an act of writing, whereby the first ray of light is a performative metaphor for that illusion of the "first" scene of inscription, its apparently inaugural, material appearance. The purpose? To edit and thus draw out of "that obscurity" the "earlier history of the public career [in which] the immortal Pickwick *would appear to be* involved." Thus writing causes to be visible that very history (in the sense of both a narrative and events of the past) that was, in being obscure, apparently subject to doubt, as the phrase *would appear to be* connotes. Boz's choice of words and phrases is interesting. It is somewhat telling and certainly more than a little ironic that in this passage on writing, illumination, obscurity, and visibility, that verb most directly to do with what one sees—*appear*—is employed equivocally, perhaps undecidably, with regard to what cannot be seen and so verified, and that this is connected to the very notion of "history." This is what appears to be illuminated—perhaps.

III. Looking in Two Directions

Boz is the figure *par excellence* of our "anachronistic" contemporary. His is a figure that, in overflowing the limits of the text, dismantles the frame and all simple stable considerations of inside/outside or text/context. "He" both writes *to* us and writes *us.* His editorial function is in part to determine the addressee. Boz also figures the *between.* He articulates and traverses the space between the world of Pickwick and that of the reader. This is not just a spatial traversal, however. It is also temporal in its function of facilitating communication and a visualization between the posthumous past, into which he slips in the very gesture of inscribing himself as archivist, and the always-to-come of the reader, to whom Boz "speaks," as the textual machine momentarily gives the illusion of reterritorializing itself in this name. We are afforded a double perspective, then, through the agency of Boz, which illuminates difference between identities and cultural manifestations of historical locations. As Juliet McMaster has observed, "it has often been noticed that *Pickwick Papers* celebrates the good old coaching days; the many coaches that figure in the narrative (many of them overturning) . . . all testify to a certain nostalgia for a mouldering if not a bygone mode of travel. But *Pickwick* also celebrates the coming of the steam locomotive, though less explicitly" (1983, 609–10). McMaster's remark aside, this double vision, this attempt to look into both the past and the future, is often not noticed.

Nevertheless, double vision is an important mode of historicization, as William J. Palmer has argued of Dickens' texts in general: "As a novelist Dickens was striving for a historical vision, attempting to ride along with the movement of history, straining *to see* the past more clearly in order *to envision* the future" (1997, 94; emphasis added). Through the recurring vision of overturning coaches, Boz offers a vision of the movement of history itself; he attests to historical, material catastrophe, the passing not only of a means of transport but also a way of life expressive of a particular perception of Englishness, though he does so in a comic way. As Palmer remarks, such a vision is always "dialogic. For every shipwreck there is rescue" (171). In reading and bringing to our sight the "inconsequential" and comic crashes of the coach, Boz refuses to distinguish in *Pickwick* between "major and minor" events and so seeks to communicate the idea, however tacitly, that "nothing that has ever happened should be regarded as lost to history" (Benjamin 2003, 390). However, this is a communication that must fail, like so many communications in *Pickwick.* For while it has been argued that *The Posthumous Papers* "carries a redemptive, almost millenarian message" (Rainsford 1997, 103),[6] one in which historical discourse is a mode "always open to change, to evolution, to perfectability" (Palmer 1997, 171), humanity for Boz has not yet been redeemed, but rather this redemption remains to come. And so, according to Walter Benjamin's conception of history, the past is not yet "citable in all its moments" for the chronicler (2003, 390). Boz may turn his eyes to the past; he may wish to linger like Benjamin's angel of history. But like that angel he is driven irresistibly—if not by the winds of paradise then by the steam of the railway—into the future to which he speaks, seeking to drive his readers in that direction also. Such double vision, the act of looking in two directions at once, is intrinsic to *Pickwick*'s vision. Indeed, as William Palmer avers, "the Dickens vision begins with Mr Pickwick" (1997, 24), however short-sighted the latter may appear. We have already seen how the proper name and the microscope arrive as encoded signs that challenge our vision of the past; we should turn now to consider what they show us of that which is to come.

In the previous section, the proper name arrived in a double manner: as a figure promising and yet withholding direct illumination. In this double, or perhaps duplicitous, simultaneity, the proper name re-marked its own fictional excess and instability. With regard to the proper name, double vision marks another name in *The Pickwick Papers:* Sam/uel. I have divided the name because it already does double service and is divided in the novel, it being the forename of both Mr Pickwick and his servant. The name passes from one to the other, shuttling between the two. Yet notice its attenuated form, Sam, which is used only for, and by Sam Weller. The name is the same and yet not the same. In the contexts of the reading I am proposing for *Pickwick,* a strong reading of this particular proper name indicates that its doubling *and* division allows for a more acute focus on the questions of historically inscribed class difference illuminated by the difference between and relation of the two Samuels. There is also a generational difference marked by the iteration of the name, and with that an oblique commentary on past and future, although Sam's age is unspecified. Even in the 1820s Samuel Pickwick is middle-aged, while Sam Weller is young. Mr Pickwick is somewhat out of date, as his tights and gaiters suggest, and is often witnessed as being unequal to contemporary life. Sam, on the other hand, is modern, a man of the future. He is at home with nineteenth-century commodity culture and technology. He buys commercially produced Valentine's Day cards and a steel-nibbed pen, and refers to artificially illuminated compound microscopes.

Pushing the strong reading of the name further, its very truncation is suggestive of the increasing speed of modern life. While the shared name, when considered as moving from one generation to another, implies a passage or even a transition of sorts, the shortening of the name connotes a discontinuity. The proper name is thus somewhat improper, its iterability announcing the written sign's ability to outlive the individual it names. The proper name reveals itself as a fiction, as was remarked of Mr Pickwick's full title earlier. The name is all that remains of Mr Pickwick and his posthumous papers, but its temporal waywardness does not await his death, his becoming posthumous. As *The Posthumous Papers of the Pickwick Club* allows us to see, it is already partially translated as *Sam,* or even *Samivel.* The shift between generations and classes is marked with a visible abruptness. Conventionally, of course, when we see the name we may believe we "see" the character, but what we see is that "we are already in writing with proper names," as Geoffrey Bennington has put it (1993, 106). In writing, Boz informs us, the subject arrives but is always already split. This general axiom of writing is clearly enacted in the doubling and transference detailed here. However, what is specifically remarked and brought into focus in this singular instance of the proper name *Sam/uel* is the fact that, as with those other examples already given, we find ourselves witnessing, yet again, the play of, and between, two distinct historicized moments of Englishness, as well as two distinct historicized modalities of representation for which the proper name is merely an encrypted figure. The arrival of the name takes place "by erasing itself . . . it comes only in its erasure" (Derrida 1987, 360). It is *simultaneously* the visibility of that erasure and the name's arrival that bears the traces of past and present, of both identity's singularity and its translatability. In a particularly graphic manner, therefore, Boz disrupts identity and meaning from within through the performative demonstration of how "naming does violence to the supposed unicity it is supposed to respect . . . the proper name depropriates, exappropriates" (Bennington 1993, 106).

The translatability of the name in *Pickwick* reveals both the materiality, the historicity of the sign and, with that recognition, the impossibility of assigning meaning. Meaning can never be guaranteed precisely because translation announces temporal and spatial transport. Such translation effects and the disturbances within the field of vision they produce arrive to sign *Pickwick* everywhere. The name is just one more example of visible doubling and distortion that occurs. In that slight passage between *Samuel* and *Sam* we witness in this small yet profoundly resonant gesture an example of what Michel Foucault has called "the irruptive violence of time" (1973, 132), which no archiving or ordering can control. In the transport of the proper name the signature of the past shuttles into the present, but at the same time emerges iterably in ruins, and in an act of revenance from within the other signature, that of the always-already-coming future *now.* And that proper name as trace of the past arrives not as some authority but as the other of the present name, its countersignature. That which we call the past survives but never as itself. What are the ramifications for *The Pickwick Papers*? As William J. Palmer, amongst many critics, observes, the text becomes "Sam Weller's novel" (1997, 35). Weller's arrival is moreover a sign that the "comedy of meaning . . . as an analogue for human inadequacy" and the "always erroneous" quest for—or assertion of—meaning that structures *Pickwick* is never merely symbolic, as Palmer asserts (32); it is also inescapably the sign of historical transformation, of the becoming of new identities materializing out of and traced by, even as they transform, the old. That the name passes from the older generation to the younger suggests the illusion of a patrilinear transference. It is, however, just an illusion; for the transference is one marked by a somewhat dialogic discontinuity between innocence and experience (which between *Samuel* and *Sam* inverts the conventional order of the knowledgeable father and the naïve son), and between masculine identities of the middle and working classes.

But then the proper name has been unstable from the very beginning of the novel, if not before. *Pickwick* is variously:

(1) the name appended to a collection of heterogeneous, posthumous papers. It is affixed as the hypothesis that drives all fiction. It serves to authorize *as if* it could provide coherence with regard to meaning, property, and propriety. Through the signatory gesture, it promises to guarantee an identity, which is never kept once the novel is recognized as Weller's, not Pickwick's. The application of the proper name *Pickwick* also admits inadvertently to the

condition of becoming posthumous inherent in the material remains of the papers and the logic of writing.

(2) the name of the club, no longer in existence.

(3) the proper name for the figure of benevolence and a tendency toward miscommunication and misinterpretation. In this, the name announces its own untrustworthiness as guarantor or authority. It authorizes only its own inability to authorize. *Pickwick* admits its own failure to remain in place; it unseats itself in the very attempt to consign the various adventures, documents, tales, and events to a proper location or indeed the assumption of any location, identity, or ontology. The only "thing" that the name *Pickwick* does authorize—and this is implicated in its always being associated with both papers and the posthumous—is its being seen and so called a trace; that which, as Derrida reminds us, "does not let itself be summed up in the simplicity of a present" (Derrida 1998, 66).

The temporal shift between *Samuel* and *Sam* would therefore appear to be inevitable. The encrypted historicity of the gesture may be admitted if we acknowledge the extent to which Dickens, as William Palmer has it, is "acutely aware that history involves much more than the events and personalities of its master texts; that history cannot just bull its way toward the future, ignorant of that culture, marginalized voices, modes of expression, and subtexts that lie beneath, and contribute to, that master text of history." Dickens is thus to be apprehended as a novelist "who 'decenters' the portrayal of history in his fiction." Furthermore, as Palmer concludes, Dickens "forms a benevolent philosophy of history" inherited in part from the texts of the eighteenth century, specifically those of Fielding, Sterne, Goldsmith, and Shaftesbury, "that functions as a fulcrum between the past and the future" (Palmer 1997, 4). More than a fulcrum, the philosophy that finds its fullest, if satirical expression in "Boz" is an optical device. In the transference of the proper name there is thus signed what Paola Marrati defines as "the deconstruction of the privilege of the present . . . and perhaps above all the classical idea of time as a *homogenous and successive* modification of the present" (2005, 125). The structural and spatial dislocation of *Pickwick,* the name, anticipates the irreversible temporal movement in Sam/uel. The processes of doubling and iterability figure in the materiality of the letter the visible signs of history's material shifts and thus open to our view the appearance of the trace, its bringing into focus the recognition of its "always-already-thereness" (Marrati 2005, 125).

Not unreasonably, Boz's use of the proper name might be described as *epochal:* not merely because in various encoded ways it can be seen to mark its own historical transitional moment, but also because, in the act of tracing such moments, it suspends any simple point of view, by complicating and therefore questioning the truth of its own evidence, albeit implicitly. It may well be the case that "*Pickwick Papers* is a high-spirited *reflection* of early Victorian class and gender relations," as J. Hillis Miller avers (emphasis added). And, as he continues, "[i]t represents a wide range of English institutions and forms of behaviour, along with the languages employed by them—languages scientific, historical, journalistic, political, legal and so forth; even including the language of hunting and cricket." Yet, as he asserts, "*Pickwick Papers* also brings into the open these elements' absurdity and their potential for causing harm. It . . . puts in question the repertoire of features making up English ideology at the moment of Victoria's accession to the throne" (Miller 1995, 131). While, following Raymond Williams, I would not be in a hurry to assign the fluidity of traces the identity of an ideology, I would nonetheless agree with Miller's assessment, adding that what makes the representation of such moments and the larger visions of Englishness that they offer to represent so absurd is their anachrony, that textual astigmatism to which our attention is drawn so silently yet graphically in the anamorphic gap of a decade, between the *then* of Pickwick and the *now* of Boz; or, to put this differently, between the *then* of *Samuel* and the *now* of *Sam.* That cultural identity is put into question at the same time as it comes to be represented is one sign of the text's material intervention in its histories. If epochal suspension takes place it is at least in part through the appearance of the anachronic trace and its force to call into question the validity of a particular period's signs.

The question of seeing, and of how one is enabled to see, is caught up with the very moment of inscription, as well as with the matter of temporality and historical location, then. Yet it has to be insisted that seeing is always a reading, a doubling that separates, as Miller's commentary on the simultaneous mapping and questioning of early Victorian culture on Dickens' part clarifies. If such "double vision" inevitably takes place within a single moment, event, or name, how much more potentially disquieting is this effect when a little time has passed? It is this truth perhaps that Boz implicitly recognizes. The further we are from an event, the less we can see without some intermediary, which always runs the risk of distorting or occluding as much as it reveals. If the problem of the present for the novel is a historical problem, then, it is precisely because the present cannot retain its presence. As many critics now acknowledge, the past is always unavailable; it does not exist *as such*. Spectacle, that is to say, the historical event, can only be witnessed once.

However, as Miller's reading and our analysis of the proper name shows, a double reading is inevitable, given the signs that remain. Evidence of this is presented by Sam at the trial of Mr Pickwick. It may not be the evidence that the prosecution desires or that the Law requires, but having to do with sight, vision, and optical prosthesis it is undeniably significant. In his strategic defense of Mr Pickwick, Sam may well have one eye on the past as that past is embodied in his master, but he clearly has an eye to the future in his reference to that invention of the late 1830s, the patent double million magnifying gas microscope, the then latest advance on Hooke's diminishing glass.[7] His words are worth repeating:

> "Yes, I have a pair of eyes," replied Sam, "and that's just it. If they wos a pair o' patent double million magnifyin' gas microscopes of hextra power, p'raps I might be able to see through a flight o' stairs and a deal door; but bein' only eyes, you see, my wision's limited." (*PP* 464)

As Boz says of Counsel's opening statements (but applicable to this moment), "A visible effect [is] produced immediately" (*PP* 450). Strictly speaking, though, it is impossible for Sam to refer to the gas microscope. At the time of the trial it had not yet been invented. Thus the remark is obviously anachronistic. Within the narrative chronology of the novel, it is a somewhat spectral trace arriving from—and perhaps offering a view of—the future. Of course, common sense tells us that Dickens—or Boz—is writing in 1837; and, moreover, he is—should we care to visualize the moment—writing in all probability with one of those steel- or "hard-nibbed pen[s] warranted not to splutter" (*PP* 431), such as the one purchased by Sam in chapter 32, which at the time of the purchase (the 1820s) was a relatively recent invention and one gaining in popularity. Yet Sam's remark, haunted as it is by a memory that cannot be his, offers a significant interruption. Representation founders in a moment of suspension, in which we must look carefully at the question of sight before the law, and an impossible vision. Sam's glib remark concerns the limits of what one can see with the naked eye. The example of supplementary, prosthetic technology that enables otherwise impossible vision presents a hypothetical scenario—a fiction—that relates technologies of observation to evidence. The comic interjection allows the trace to draw attention to the fact that evidence presented before the Law is always implicated in a narrative, historical retrospect intended to bring before the jury a vision that they cannot have, through that agent of the gaze, the witness, the future of whom is to be supplemented, if not replaced by supposedly more reliable forensic technologies of vision. Despite the humor the anachronism is jarring; it disturbs in a strangely apposite manner. For its singular arrival serves to remark that all reading and writing are structured, indeed are only possible, through the work of such anachrony, and so are disjointed temporally, between what is seen and what is being narrated. In its utilization of sight and what will come to be one aspect of forensic technology, the vision we are vouchsafed by Sam is of a future of the Law, and its present limits to produce testimony.

That which Sam reveals more generally is the condition of narrative and its projected phantasms as being, in John Bowen's words, "something strange, belated, and secondary" (2000, 51). Stepping outside the frame of this particular scene in order to risk a hypothesis on perspective once more, it is *as if* the patent double million magnifying gas microscope "returns" from the future in order to illuminate, illustrate, and magnify not only the present limits of the law but also the motions of Boz's steel-nibbed pen in its projection of a phantom past, *as if* that were present. Yet in the very same moment, because the microscope *cannot* be there, the very idea of a present is materially and historically problematized from within the very scene itself, and thus evidence—specifically evidence concerning what can and cannot be seen, what has or has not been witnessed—is shown to be unreliable, faulty. The Law relies on sight, but sight cannot be proven. Ironically, a complex structure is revealed even as it is dismantled before our very eyes, as it were—by which we are always haunted, and which we have yet to envision in all its complexity. As Sam makes plain, the Law cannot produce or command presence; its power only ever opens up a seeing in two directions and a double vision. For as Sam's testimony lets us see all, *Pickwick*'s vision is always just this doubling, this split and the play of difference in the historicity's representation of "a present image of an absent thing," wherein "the absent thing itself gets split into disappearance into and existence in the past" (Ricoeur 2004, 280). But this properly "historical condition," as Ricoeur has it, is not only a matter of the "having been" as "being no longer." *Pickwick*'s vision admits that the "being no longer" can also produce a vision of that which is to come. This is its hope, the hope that we may come to envision as being signalled between Samuel and Sam.

Afterword

The Old Story . . . with a Difference

The time for reflection is also a chance for turning back on the very conditions of reflection, in all senses of that word, *as if* with the help of a new optical device one could finally see sight, could not only view the natural landscape, the city, the bridge, and the abyss, but could "view" viewing. . . . Then the time of reflection is also an other time; it is heterogeneous to what it reflects . . .
—Jacques Derrida, "The Principle of Reason: The University in the Eyes of its Pupils" (2004)

And yet the more I think about Dickens, the less I think that "narrative," in the ordinary sense, is a good way of describing his mode. The word that insistently suggests itself is "presentation." For there is an unusual *mobility* in this narrator. He moves from place to place and from the point of view of one character after another, with much more diversity than any other novelists of his time . . . he can establish at a break a new mode. There is nothing of the uniformity of narrative of the classic realist text. And there is something else which I don't know if we have the terms for . . . a crucial variable in the question of realist fiction . . . an element of Dickens's writing . . . is subjunctive, which is clearly "what if" or "would that" or "let us suppose that." In other words, he introduces a perspective which is not socially or politically available. It is a hypothesis of a perspective, a feeling, a force, which he knows not to be in the existing balance of forces that was there to be observed.
—Raymond Williams, *Writing in Society* (1983)

And when it is accomplished—behold!—all the truth of life is there: a moment of vision, a sigh, a smile—and the return to an eternal rest.
—Joseph Conrad, "Preface," *The Nigger of the "Narcissus"* (1897)

I. Pronouncing Parallax

In focusing throughout this study on the odd, insistent recurrence of figures of sight, vision, visualization, and so on in *Pickwick,* I have situated a series of questions that arise in part from a struggle with determination similar to that expressed by Raymond Williams in the second of my three epigraphs (1983, 160–61), fragments of which have already surfaced in previous chapters. Though already asked, and in part answered, they should now be restated. Why do these motifs, figures, metaphors, and forms of *seeing* occur and recur, and why do they keep coming and going, taking place in that *now* of the novel's publication in the 1830s? What, if anything, have the various figures of the visible to do with the act of narration, and, specifically, narration—and by extension the novel—as it undergoes transformation in the early nineteenth century as a result of external forces affecting modes of literary production? What do the visual and visible, sight and observation have to do with that strange notion of "history," or with historical event, date, or fact, especially in the very singular example of a text that might best be described as articulating "historicity without history—historicity without reference to actual occurrences but only exposure of its field" (Fenves 1993, 76)? What is the novel's relationship both to its present and its pasts, to the histories of the culture from which it arrives, and how? Finally, a question that, though not asked, is implicit in the conclusion of the last chapter: if, like Sam Weller, we only have eyes, albeit a pair, how can we "see" and so bear witness to that which is no longer available to our view, without the aid of some technology? The answer to this last question is of course that we cannot, nor do we ever, simply see. As *The Pickwick Papers* makes blindingly obvious, there is no sight without either the possibility of interpretive interruption, translative interference, or some form of prosthesis, most simply understood as the act of interpretation or translation itself. Any sight claiming unmediated veracity is to be distrusted if only because there is no single perspective, as all the examples of eyes watching other eyes watching others inform us.

Though he struggles to find the right words and admits as much in a vulnerable critical gesture of reflective self-reading, Raymond Williams perceives the "problem" of Dickens in the epigraph above in a way that is markedly more clear-sighted than many subsequent materialist or historicist readers of Dickens. Unlike those who forget that the time of reflection is heterogeneous to what is reflected and so, perhaps, see only a strange reflection of themselves that they misperceive as the figure in (or *of*) the Dickensian text, Williams apprehends in his grasping after the proper language the opening of a temporal and spatial network composed and discomposed by multifarious lines of sight. The motions within this weave produce a performative presentation, a visionary staging rather than a merely constative narrative in Dickens in general, but arguably particularly in *Pickwick.* The "subjunctive" perspective that finds its appearance most obviously in those hypothetical spectators and observers but also in the redirection of the reader's gaze toward another line of sight in any given scene opens the point of view from within itself to the perspective of the other.

This visionary structure is formulated by Kant in "Dreams of a Visionary Explained by Dreams of Metaphysics." "Formally," Kant reflects, "I viewed human common sense only from the standpoint of my own; now," he continues, in language that admits of the temporal disjunction inherent in the act of seeing oneself seeing,

> I put myself into the position of another's reason outside of myself, and observe my judgements, together with their most secret causes, from the point of view of others. It is true that the comparison of both observations results in pronounced parallaxes, but it is the only means of preventing the optical delusion, and of putting the concept of the power of knowledge in human nature into its true place. (Kant 1993, 15)

While not suggesting that Dickens had any knowledge of Kant, nonetheless when taking *Pickwick* together with the Kantian text, the visual structures of the former come to be refocused in a particularly sharp manner by the insights of the latter. That Dickensian subjunctive, the *what if,* echoes the Kantian *as if* (*als ob*), whereby through the spectral agency of analogy the imagination is vouchsafed a vision otherwise unavailable. In *Pickwick*'s vision the spatial displacements and temporal disjunctions that inform the structure of envisioning only operate through the pronounced "parallax" of Boz's mediation. Distortion and doubling take place, but do so as the means whereby optical delusion is prevented in the interests of presenting to the reader's view the text's historicity as that optical device for giving access to self-reading *from the point of view of others. Pickwick* sees sight and thus opens the reader's eyes not only to the sight of the recently passed, rapidly receding past, but also to the matter of how one might view that past: with one eye for sentiment and another, which in glancing through the temporal astigmatism of cynicism, parody, and satire allows for the possibility of reflecting upon one's own identity, occasionally looking to the future also. As Lindsay Smith has argued, "vision is imaginatively powerful;

it enables forms of imaginative contemplation, the articulation of memory, and speculative projection. Vision allows us to occupy other times and spaces." In foregrounding repeatedly the implicitly temporal and historical gap at work in "binocular dissimilarity" rather than resolving "two images into one" (Smith 1995, 4) Boz puts into play those forms of double vision we have sought to illustrate and illuminate. In coming to see this, we may also suggest provisionally that it is *as if* in the febrile oscillations that the editor machine sets in motion, *Pickwick*'s vision mediates a broader cultural "fascination with perceptual aberration" and the observable obsession in nineteenth-century visual theory across the discourses of aesthetics, psychology, and science with "vision gone awry" (Smith 1995, 5).

The problem of vision is not only historical or cultural, though. When mediated by the literary text, it admits also in the perception of "aberrations" of translation its uncontrollable effects produced by the anachrony of the trace. Boz admits as much in a dialogue between Mr Pickwick and Mr Perker: "'it's the old story I suppose?' 'With a difference, my dear Sir; with a difference,' rejoined Perker, deliberately folding up the paper and putting it in his pocket again" (*PP* 624; once more a scene of eyes, gazes, Mr Perker being observed "glancing eagerly at Mr Pickwick out of the corners of his eyes"; a scene also of narrative, reading, and writing). Through the limits of the eyewitness and the supplementary necessity and failure or untrustworthiness of narrative as belated envisioning, Sam's affirmation of a technology to come to which we were witnesses at the end of the last chapter acknowledges indirectly and by a kind of analogical apperception the conditions by which we see the past, if we see it at all. Being able to see the past at all is to tell the old story with a difference, and to acknowledge the hypothesis of a perspective—*as if one could see.* This is the very condition by which any perception of historicity is possible as, in its own way, the title of *The Pickwick Papers* gives us to understand. We come to see that the novel for Boz is another form of tele-technology. It produces for the reader visions no longer available to the naked eye. As the diminishing glass or compound microscope finds a world in solution, so too does Boz through *Pickwick*'s vision. The vignettes of the embedded narratives demonstrate this economically. As they project themselves into the foreground and the present moment of the narrative, thereby suspending the present and presence through the revenance of the traces of the past, so we witness the event and, simultaneously, we are *in* the experience. Writing, as a form of tele-technology or telecommunication that enables the transition from the invisible to the visible, brings about the transition from empirical absence to virtual, specular, and spectral presence.

In an odd fashion the figure of the patent double million magnifying gas microscope allows us to see this, as should now be clear. It fictionalizes Sam's account, as the sign of a certain perjury, falsifying as it does avowal and testimony. In this, the ghostly *revenant* of technology-to-come affirms in the most indirect manner possible the work of storytelling, in the double sense of both narrating and lying.[1] All writing is thus unveiled as a fiction, a fiction concerning the projection of the visualization of the impossible; *Pickwick* pursues this thread, weaving itself endlessly between the textual and visual image. As Peter Schwenger has it of narrative, there is a constant "switching between verbal and imagistic codes," and readers must shuttle between verbal and visual systems (1999, 47, 48). While Schwenger is speaking of the act of reading in general, and, implicitly, the concomitant act of writing that produces what he calls a phantasmic "*effect* of existence" (49), *Pickwick*'s specific and singular textual loom is one that weaves in a process of constant loss and gain, two distinct sign systems as we have already affirmed, comprising what is seen and what is written. Both announce the instability of perception so that, to cite Schwenger once more, "in a perceptual hide and seek we lose the word to find the image, lose the image in the word. Reading [and writing also, in the example of Dickens with which we are interested], it seems, proceeds in rhythms, risings and fallings and alterations of perceptions" (1999, 59–60).

Writing is a fiction, a tele-technological medium of hypothetical perspectives and analogical visualization. Through its structural relationship to absence (of a being, of beings, of the past), it announces itself as a vehicle of translation that is not only spatial but also inescapably, indelibly temporal. Writing is, here and there, then and now—and *now*—but never as an absolute present or presence. It is thus always a reminder of its own supplementary status. If from a certain perspective this is well known for some critics, it seems necessary that we remind ourselves of the point and not lose sight of its significance on the premise or unjustifiable excuse that such critical ideas have had their day, that they are past, in the past, where they should remain and not resurface. Despite the critical desire to forget (itself a kind of performative gesture), we have to remember and so to see clearly that writing is *both* survival *and* death. Writing thus operates through a very specific kind of fiction, that of analogical envisioning caught in the phrase *as if: as if,* for example, we could see or visit, or have returned to us, the 1820s; as if Mr Pickwick and his friends were, if not alive, then having the capacity at least of returning briefly as ghostly illuminations through the spirit-medium of the "editor effect" or editorial projection machine. As Jacques Derrida has remarked, "the *as if,* the fiction, the *quasi-*, these are what protect us from the real event of death itself, if such a thing exists" (Derrida 1996b, 217). Boz's acknowledgment of this condition of writing as visionary tele-technology is there from the title onward, even as that title reminds us that we are always in a relationship to the written word akin to, analogous with, a motion of becoming visible. At the same time, however, the fiction of the *as if* that "protects" us is double. For it reminds us that we are implicated in this double movement—of becoming visible as the anticipated trace of becoming posthumous. Here, we might suggest, is one of the many signs of *The Pickwick Papers'* historicity and the historicity of its vision, in its acknowledgment of the graphic condition of our being's temporality. The modernity of *The Pickwick Papers,* that modernity we now name Victorian, is signalled in its acknowledgment of the materiality and temporality of being. If we receive the novel at all, we receive it not simply as a collection of comic misadventures, but also as a heterogeneous collection of *memento mori.* In order to see this, let us turn to one last moment of vision at the heart of *The Posthumous Papers of the Pickwick Club.*

II. The Ghosts of Christmas Past, Present, and to Come

At the structural center of *The Posthumous Papers* is chapter 28 (there are 56 chapters). This is "A good-humoured Christmas Chapter, containing an account of a Wedding, and some other Sports beside, which although in their way, even as good customs as Marriage itself, are not quite so religiously kept up, in these degenerate times" (*PP* 360–90). That the title draws our attention to customs and degenerate times implies that the old story is very much transformed by temporal difference. We should also note that the chapter is a scene of both Christmas and marriage celebration, suggestive of an implicit double vision, having to do with remembrance of things past on the one hand and visions of life to come on the other. Though not the only tale concerned with Christmas in *Pickwick,* this particular presentation of the season is the most significant. As with the case of "The Story of the Bagman's Uncle" and many, if not all, of the revenant tales of *Pickwick* that "enact a work of remembrance, particularly of the dead" (Bowen 2000, 76), the work of writing is revealed once more as a tele-technology, a new optical device, which brings before our eyes many haunting figures and memories otherwise unavailable and invisible so that we are translated, coming to inhabit two locations simultaneously.

In this chapter is "The Story of the Goblins who stole a Sexton" (*PP* 380–90). To recall the words of John Bowen, if *Pickwick* is "a fictional economy" structured by "impulse, excess, and misdirection," then chapter 28 is a concentrated and excessively singular example of this fictional economy. The Christmas chapter is marked by references to sight, to eyes, and to vision as well, even as it plays with and on the by-now-familiar tropes of *Pickwick.* Verbal misunderstanding announces the failure of communication (*PP* 365; "what I mean is . . ."). Equivocation concerning perception and its subsequent narrative approximation mocks picturesque convention: "grey twilight (slate-coloured is a better term)" (*PP* 366). Zeugma returns once more: "All the girls were in tears and white muslin" (*PP* 369). There are also instances of temporal narrative iterability, when on one occasion Boz recalls that "they had travelled over *nearly* the same ground on a previous occasion" (*PP* 364; emphasis added) and on another Wardle says of Joe, *yet again,* "damn that boy, he's gone to sleep" (*PP* 370). Before "The Story of the Goblins" Sam tells a tale (*PP* 375), and the reader is presented the text of a song, "A Christmas Carol" (*PP* 378–79), the graphic appearance of which announces the disjunction between what is seen and what is heard. The double moment of the song highlights the different times of experience and event that *Pickwick* has been at pains to highlight elsewhere.

The various linguistic disruptions that call the reader's attention to problems of perception, literal or metaphorical, aside, the interpolated tale of the Goblins is not exempt from visual figures. The tale, concerning the alleged abduction of Gabriel Grub, the sexton of the title, anticipates Dickens' *Christmas Carol* in certain respects, not least in the visions that appear to Grub at the command of the Goblin King, who pokes Gabriel in the eye (*PP* 386–89). Why mention this gesture? It seems as if the Goblin King is seeking to draw Grub's attention to his own moral myopia and blinding self-interest in this manner. "[B]eing spirits," the goblins "leave no *visible* impression" (*PP* 389). The figure "he saw" is reiterated five times in a single paragraph (*PP* 388–89) as commentary on Grub's role as spectator and witness to the phantasmic visions of the work, the joys, and the suffering of humanity. The spectral nature of the scenes alerts the reader to the fact that Grub is both witness to the experience and in the experience itself, to recall from chapter 2 Rosalind Krauss' discussion of the uncanny effect on the subject of the zoetrope. At the same time, however, Grub's subject position is also that implicitly of the reader of *The Pickwick*

Papers. Moving on, Grub's subsequent abduction is "not wanting some very credible *witnesses* who had *seen* him whisked through the air on the back of a chestnut horse *blind of one eye . . .*" (*PP* 389; emphasis added). Yet despite all this, the fact that the historical moment of the story has long since receded and that this is yet one more retelling, it is remarked that "in the course of time it began to be received as a matter of history, in which form it has continued down to this very day" (*PP* 390). Sentiment, as subjective awareness, feeling, or impression, can, in the form of narration, take on the force of historical truth. However, it is not individual sentiment that enacts the transformation of the narrative. Rather, there is a collective sentiment, given expression as the cultural collective memory of the story.

It is *as if* the chapter is constructed as both a series of narrative frames embedded within one another and as an endless temporal loop of images. It is as if narrative aspired to the condition of phantom zoetrope, figuring in itself an impossible and excessive structure replaying over and over an excessive phantasmagoria of tropes and images, in an act of hospitality and remembrance. Each structure, each projection, invites us to *see.* Yet as a preface to the scenes of celebration, we read the following passage:

> We write these words now, many miles distant from the spot on which, *year after year,* we met on that day, a *merry and joyous circle.* Many of the hearts that throbbed so gaily then, have ceased to beat; many of the *looks* that shone so brightly then, have ceased to glow; the hands we grasped, have grown cold; the *eyes* we sought, have hid their lustre in the grave; yet the old house, the room, the merry voices and smiling *faces,* the jest, the laugh, the most minute and trivial circumstance connected with those happy meetings, crowd upon our mind at each *recurrence* of the season, *as if* the last assemblage had been but yesterday. (*PP* 359; emphasis added)

The initial shift to present tense in the opening clause of the sentence accompanies a reflective acknowledgment of the act of writing. In a constant flux between past and present, "in which every perception is already memory" (Bergson 1999, 150), we move, "we" shuttle, between loss and gain, absence and the numerous phantom presences that "crowd upon our mind" with every temporal reiteration. The motion is also caught in both the shift from *now* to *then* and *then,* in its motion from *looks* to *eyes* to *faces,* and in the circular and temporal movements of the annual cycle and the recurrence of gathering. (One might also catch in the more obscure echoes of *circumstance* the motion of surrounding that encircles and gathers together the fragmented images in a gesture of connection.) The good reader will note the syllepsistic doubling in the first sentence. The temporal recirculation of *year after year* finds itself doubled in the image of the *merry and joyous circle,* which figure exceeds its own image of the gathering of friends to announce the refolding of time past and time future in the constant slippage of the otherwise invisible time present briefly apprehended in that figure *we. Our* perception, *our* memory—which is to say not only the memory that might be ours but also the memory of ourselves—finds itself interwoven into that "multitude of remembered elements" (Bergson 1999, 150) that the citation performs as well as observes, through the inaugural, self-reflexive affirmation that *we write these words now.* Attention to the present yet ephemeral moment of the graphic mark as trace admits even that "our consciousness of the present is already memory" (151).

The passage thus proceeds as the inscription of visionary memory, through which, though "we" remember now, "we" are projected back to the memory of "our presence" in that company. It is not only *as if* the scenes had occurred, but also *as if* we were part of the "assemblage"—which in effect *we* become, in being written into the phantasy scenario. There is thus produced an overlaying of supposedly discrete times in the trope and motion of circularity. Through the vision of assemblage a composition of eyes, faces, hands, voices, looks, and laughter becomes visible as itself an assemblage of momentary visions. While the first appearance of Mr Pickwick in the novel's opening chapter had been the occasion of that *tableau vivant,* designed to promote the illusion of Mr Pickwick *as if* he were alive, here a singular image of multiple moments comes into focus through its unfixed temporal motion. Writing's spectral projection, with its power to produce visions, moves in several directions at once, to produce a sight more real than any empirical evidence could suggest. The spirit of the past is maintained here, through the sentiment of awareness and feeling, rather than any crass sentimentality. And this is so because, for this brief, ever-present epoch, structured through tense and pronoun, we "appear" to ourselves, as *we* share, we are interpellated in a community of death. For this is not only a Christmas past, it is also the spirit of every Christmas to come. In the act of writing *we* the novel comes to confront its own imaginary. At the abyssal heart of the novel, memory, vision, and the materiality of the letter, given a phantasmic subjectivity through the editorial projection of *we,* come together in a performative projection, an "oratorical visualization" (de Bolla 1989, 292).

In this instant, therefore, *Pickwick* does not allow for the reading of

Christmas as a "sentimental utopia," as John Bowen has argued (2000, 80). Such an act of memory, which is also an act of mourning, as the passage makes clear with its references to those who are dead, demands that we keep alive an ethical commitment to bearing witness, in excess of any mere historical record. Writing relies on the very phantoms that it conjures, in the articulation of what Alessia Ricciardi describes (with reference to the films of Pier Paolo Passolini) as the "mournful imagination" of a writer "determined to offer hospitality to an array of . . . spectralized subjects." This suggests in turn in this particular instance a "politics of the hospitality to the Other. . . . Even melancholia is a form of hospitality to a fundamental Otherness" (Ricciardi 2003, 126). Why should such structures of visualization appear significant? What can the spectral vision tell us of history and the past that empirical evidence and textual representation confined by mimetic verisimilitude cannot? In excess of the pragmatic or empirical demands and limits of fiction writing and the guilty social conscience, by which such writing would appear to be motivated in the face of its own inability to do anything other than *look,* Boz's text relies on, and risks, the resonance of a phenomenology of sentiment in its hospitality. For, in being open to the spectacle of the phantom other, it opens the possibility for envisioning what is to come. Through his "phantasmagorical vision of culture" (Ricciardi 2003, 128), Boz offers a way out of a certain historical impasse by which fiction, the novel, narrative might otherwise be bound. As the memory of Christmas suggests, a mournful reverie is perhaps the most appropriate mode, in this example at least, by which the writer may be haunted by history, and by which writing may produce visions to which future readers may themselves bear witness. Haunted by the traces of others, Boz responds by producing his own trace. In projecting visions of the past in which the ghosts of the "present" announced through the plural pronoun return to the scene of the past from its future, Boz disappears into a trace available "if not for everyone, at least for others" (Derrida 2005, 24). Attestation thus becomes, or is traced by, a gesture of confession, in this instance of one's own temporality and finitude. Boz's act of speaking *of* and *to* the other, in bearing witness to what cannot be witnessed except through the visionary and analogical indirection of language, thus betrays the other "by the fact that it is already mediated in . . . a general language which is not a unique signature" (Derrida 2005, 24). But it does so through the inevitable revenance of the trace that in its historicity makes *Pickwick*'s vision of past times possible.

From this understanding, it might be said that *The Posthumous Papers of the Pickwick Club* thus arrives as an encrypted and interiorized vision of many of the traces of English culture. The visualization of the Christmas gathering with its interpolated tales and other heterogeneous elements serves not so much to project a specifically Christian, redemptive image as to attest to the becoming posthumous of one particular manifestation of national culture and identity, in which the Anglo-Christian trace is to be read as one amongst many. Phantasmic visualization, and with that the poetics of the *as if* that enables the projection of the image, allows the alterity of the other to be glimpsed, while also making possible not a reflection but rather a metonymic or analogical identification. This can be *seen* and *read* at work in that performative, reflective figure of the *most minute and trivial circumstance* observed by Boz above, which enables the possibility of connection. It does so because the *circum-* of circumstance announces and thus re-marks not only the recirculation of cyclical revenance but also the cut, the mark of the trace that announces the historicity and singularity of the material *circumstance* that can never return as it was. Thus the editor and translation effects of which we have spoken risk witness and betrayal in order to maintain the mediation of a binocular dissimilarity and distortion by which iterable communication has its chance. In this, *The Posthumous Papers* affirms literature's responsibility to bear witness to those traces of the past that are, and remain, "as inaccessible as [they are] ineluctable" (Derrida 2001, 144). And literature's power arrives—or has the merest chance of arriving, supposing it might be received—in that endless motion between the verbal and the visual, in what Derrida has called "imaginal transfiguration," which is "from the very start fantastic or phantasmic: under certain conditions, of course, and this is the central problem of the pragmatic conditions of such efficacity; all history is at issue here" (2001, 151). In privileging the phantasmic over the empirical image, in exposing the instability of language in its generation of meaning, Dickens acknowledges the extent to which history is at issue, and demands that we *feel* responsible, that we *feel* accountable.[2] In this chance, there might come, perhaps to the mind's eye, or in the blink of an eye, the responsibility of mourning and memory in excess of and in response to any supposed control or mastery over the representation of events, whether of any present or any past.

III. Inventing *Pickwick*

I return to one of my starting points. Like Samuel Pickwick I return to where I began—but, it is to be hoped, with a difference. It is a commonplace amongst critics of Dickens that *Pickwick* is readable as part imitation, part pastiche, of older literary magazines, collections of miscellanies, and their subject matter. There is nothing new in acknowledging this. What is significant in the manner of appearance of *The Pickwick Papers* is that it signals and belongs to a transformation in literary interests. As Kathryn Chittick has noted, "that Dickens first appeared in the pages not of a quarterly—he was never cultured enough even later for that—but of a monthly is a faithful reflection of a mid-century for which Dickens is sometimes glowingly given single-handed credit" (1990, 329). Yet I would aver that the extent to which Boz tells the old story with a difference remains to be considered fully, grounded as commentary on sources and influences has been for the most part on intertextual and formal analysis. Boz mocks or otherwise troubles the very forms and genres he employs, thereby signalling a distance from older modes of production, older narrative interests and structures, thereby announcing an instant of literary and cultural becoming.

One symptom of such invention readable as the signs of "becoming Victorian" or "becoming modern" is that self-conscious distanciation we have sought to address. The mode of becoming is registered in that *presentation* of which Raymond Williams hesitatingly speaks. It marks itself in its difference from its other and thus from its *pasts. The Pickwick Papers* is readable as performing for its reader a countersignature to the histories of both the text and the reader. This gesture wagers materially on similarity *and* difference, tradition *and* innovation. In this fashion a distance is inscribed, an unsuturable temporal gap opened, across which nevertheless pass the phantoms of the past, invented as shared, transmissible memories and visions. As *Pickwick* informs us, one of the ways in which this takes place is through a reading practice that aims at being subversive or ironic, thereby destabilizing meanings and identities that conventional wisdom has told us we should accept.

In order to see this more clearly, let us compare *Pickwick* with another novel that expresses the Romantic vision of the past and its attempted retrieval of the traces of history. While Ann Radcliffe's *A Sicillian Romance* expresses an "impulse to retrieve the past . . . assisted by the conventions of the picturesque whereby a critical and creative human spectator discovers harmony" (Stabler 2002, 5), *Pickwick* counters such convention through the foregrounding of "discordant elements" in the field of vision and thus marks its distance from outmoded forms of cultural consensus. Such consensus relied on an implicit understanding of an "unspoken, but precise, set of social or cultural circumstances" (Stabler 2002, 5), which are seen in *Pickwick* as no longer coherent and yet which persist in their return to mark the text—and, by implication the present moment of the reader. Furthermore, in contrast to the conventions of sentimental travel writing there is in *Pickwick* a repeated failure to observe "the eighteenth-century conventions . . . [involving] the encounter between two feeling individuals [engaged in] an exchange of intelligence, benevolence and civilised communication" (Stabler 2002, 5). Whether by "communication" we allude to discussion or anachronistic modes of transport, it is clear that for Boz and his readers the conventions no longer hold and are there only to be satirized and subverted.

The permanent parabasis of irony by which Boz communicates between the ruins of a past and the ghosts of the future also signals the pronounced parallax involved in seeing from differing points of view. It admits that the temporal space of the decade between the imagined events of *Pickwick* and their editorial re-presentation is porous, as are those spaces between the text and the subsequent times of its reading. Consequently, it has to be observed that something overflows the historical moment or context and any simple perception of it, doing so in an immaterial way. Arriving at another moment the excessive trace can cause a material effect in my reading that I cannot control, and which, furthermore, I cannot explain, even though I may believe that I *see.* As we have seen in the endless spectral circling of the circumstances of Christmas, the trace travels, but is never intact. As one of those *remains* of the old story that *remain,* it *remains* though never as itself; it thus *remains* to be read.[3] "History" is at best, then, itself a permeable and problematic concept, and perhaps no longer even maintainable as a concept. The past transmits and continues to transmit signals that *parasitize,* inhabiting and haunting their host in a strange manner. Boz's language and the images it conjures are we might say a swarm of phantoms. This is what *Pickwick*'s vision would have us *see.* In consequence, if I receive the strangeness of the text from another moment in time, if it arrives in an unforeseen manner despite institutions and conventions, this is because of a certain intensity, "the intensity," I would like to suggest, "of border-crossing memory discourses" (Huyssen 2003, 12).

This intensity, spoken of by Andreas Huyssen, offers one model of what takes place in reading *Pickwick*'s vision. It identifies the somewhat spectral process in the experience of reading literature, whether from another decade or another century. It hints at how the literary intervenes in its own cultures, its own pasts—and indeed futures. The text remains, even as we read and receive it, only as the manifestation of some ghostly arrival. And this arrival is also a return, for what returns to us are those momentarily constellated memories that have never been ours, but the images of which persist as they flash before us. As Aristotle understood, in "memory we have one kind of temporal *perception* that is oriented by what caused the affective *picture*. . . . Memory . . . constitutes . . . an awareness of pastness and past impressions" (Scott 1999, 126). If we receive such phantasms at all it is because the text refuses to remain buried as a discrete historical phenomenon, simply assignable or consignable as such. To put this differently, the spectral logic of narrative, with its differential transmission of *the old stories* and the visions they encourage through the force of difference, refuses to be assigned to dead letters or posthumous papers. As J. Hillis Miller has argued, certain texts "can't easily fit . . . into history. The best works are other to their times" (2004b, 406). *The Pickwick Papers* is one such text.

Despite its canonical status *Pickwick* remains problematic because it announces its own temporal, historical otherness as well as its relation to every other. In doing so, it dispels any cultural illusion that literature is "a medium for instantaneous and continuous transmission that would postpone the cut in communications traffic" (Siegert 1999, 248–49) announced throughout *Pickwick*. And it does so furthermore before the conventions of what have become subsequently known as classic realism have had the chance to get under way. Contrary to the motions of classic realism that appear to guarantee consistency of perspective and overview, *Pickwick* proceeds by "intervals" that place "the subject in question" (Siegert 1999, 249). Dickens' first novel thus stages an epochal suspension—that is to say, it announces nothing other than an engagement with the necessity of recognizing an inescapable encounter with fictionality, and with spectrality (Derrida 2005, 89). If it is available to our readings it is thus as other to its times and to every time. In what might be called its weak messianic hope, as envisioned through the temporal re-mark of Christmas, *Pickwick*'s vision appears to be that of "a text without end" (Siegert 1999, 249).

At the same time, *The Posthumous Papers of the Pickwick Club* also re-marks itself as being haunted by times that are not its own. Its editorial intervention in that which is posthumous is a simultaneous act of remembering and forgetting, as Sylviane Agacinski avers, in that the very gesture of "conserving the traces aids in remembering and forgetting at the same time" (2003, 89). In its very writing, *Pickwick* issues a cautionary reminder about the materiality of the literary text: despite our best efforts to decode it the text remains other, and thus remains to be read, to come. But this remainder is nothing new. As other, it announces that which is to come by folding back on the past, and enfolding the past into itself in a manner that is innovative.[4] Like Boz, we have to live with and respond to the phantoms. We have to invent *Pickwick,* producing in this act of invention a vision—one among many—of differentiated, self-differentiating cultural identities in their becoming. Invention names here not the creation of something new, unexpected, radical. Rather, invention is that which allows for the possibility—but never more than this—of the coming of the other. This cannot be programmed or predicted as a reading. At most it might be taken as a gesture of opening our eyes, thereby letting the other come in (*invenire*). *Pickwick*'s vision might teach us that if we look carefully enough. And as that vision recalls, we can only prepare for such an invention and thus wager on the occurrence of this otherwise incalculable event by telling the old story, with a difference.

Notes

Notes to Introduction

1. Derrida's coining is in part a strategic defense against the assumptions of getting to the bottom of a problem or inquiry, to speak colloquially, implicit in the idea of an archaeology. As Derrida's comprehension of the archive demonstrates, this alternative figure, when opened to its own deconstruction, is radically abyssal.

2. I take these formulae from Paul de Man. See *Rhetoric of Romanticism* (1984, 262); *The Resistance to Theory* (1986, 51); *Aesthetic Ideology* (1996, 82, 90).

3. To speak of "poststructuralist cliché" is to engage in a kind of self-reflexive performative gesture; more plainly put, such a phrase is itself a cliché that proscribes further reading (or reading at all). Such a phrase is generated by what might be called an ontological desire: a will to determine and delimit an identity of critical reading that erases the differences between and singularity of certain critical praxes in the production of a homogeneous meaning, or at least an ipseity that in all truth has not existed. But then herein lies the problem. For what I have just said might be read as all too general and, therefore, subject to interpretation, yet again, as "poststructuralist cliché." Someone therefore will have stopped reading. Certainly, they will not have seen that other things are, or could be, taking place; that, for example, there is a certain "brash" spirit behind the claims being made here (to recall the language of the series editor of the Victorian Critical Interventions Series). It must be enough for now to suggest, however brashly, that as soon as an ontology is assumed, *there* the reader, in falling into cliché or, more appropriately for this study, *stereotype,* stops reading—and therefore stops looking, stops seeing.

These comments are not simply a defense of or *apologia* for my critical practice. They are very much involved in an insistence implicit throughout *The Old Story, with a Difference* that certain modes of critical perception, however appropriate to other novels by Dickens, encounter difficulties and limits with Dickens' first novel. This insistence remains implicit for the most part because it is not my aim to criticize other critical modes per se but to note that, with regard to ways of seeing, particularly ways in which we view the past, *The Pickwick Papers* has quite a lot to show us, and to show us differently.

4. Bearing in mind the definitions of these words, having to do with particular forms of printing and the repeatability of characteristics, I shall be drawing on both concepts at appropriate moments in this study.

5. The passage from which the epigraph is taken concerns Teufelsdröch's university years, and is discussed below, in the body of the introduction.

Notes to Chapter 1

1. See Dickens, *The Dent Uniform Edition of Dickens' Journalism, Volume I: Sketches by Boz and Other Early Papers, 1833–39* (1994); *The Dent Uniform Edition of Dickens' Journalism, Volume II: The Amusements of the People and Other Papers: Reports, Essays and Reviews, 1834–1851* (1996a). A selection of Dickens' later journalism is collected in *Selected Journalism, 1850–1870* (1997). A now little-known early publication of Dickens' is *Memoirs of Joseph Grimaldi, edited by Boz* (1838), the biography of the most popular clown and pantomime artist in England.

2. On the literary and cultural interest in the "Cockney" as urban phenomenon in the 1820s and 1830s, see G. Dart, "The Cockney Moment (The Character of the Cockney in Dickens's *Pickwick Papers* and *Sketches by Boz*)" (2003). The error, that Dickens was a Cockney, aside, the article provides a significant intervention in the historicization and cultural contextualization of Dickens' first novel. While one can become a Londoner, one cannot become a Cockney. To be a Cockney, one must be born within the sound of the bells of St Mary-le-Bow, one of the first churches to be built by Sir Christopher Wren, between 1670 and 1683, after the Great Fire of London of 1666. Dickens was born in Portsmouth.

3. Of course, whether *Pickwick* is a novel has been a matter of critical contention, as my third epigraph indicates (Schlicke 1999, 450). As Schlicke points out, A. E. Dyson's *The Inimitable Dickens* (1970) "silently refrains from discussing *Pickwick*" (450). Dyson's is not the only study, however, to omit Dickens' first novel, and were there space, it might be argued that the modernity of *Pickwick* as transformation—or perhaps deconstruction—of the ontology of the novel has not yet been properly received or read. I discuss certain notable omissions or occlusions and marginalizations below, but a summary remark is offered by Grahame Smith. In his *The Novel and Society: Defoe to George Eliot* (1984), Smith comments that *Pickwick* is insusceptible "to a reading in the general terms established by the classic modern theories of the novel" (179). John Bowen comments on the problems of *Pickwick*'s form and identity for criticism, particularly the divergence between reading the novel's language and form in terms either of contingency or transcendence, in the first part of chapter 2 of his *Other Dickens* (45–51). As Bowen's notes throughout the chapter seem to indicate through the reference to critical discussions of *Pickwick* and their dates of publication, analysis of *Pickwick* decreases markedly from the 1970s onward.

There are a number of fascinating articles on Dickens' excessive pastiche-picaresque published in journals over the last quarter century, several of which I refer to in this chapter. In addition to the articles by Jonathan Grossman and

Kathryn Chittick already cited, I would direct the reader to the following: James E. Marlow, "Pickwick's Writing: Propriety and Language" (1985); Jacqueline Simpson, "Urban Legends in *The Pickwick Papers*" (1983); and Juliet McMaster, "Visual Design in *Pickwick Papers*" (1983).

On *Pickwick* see also Chittick's *Dickens and the 1830s* (1990); Steven Connor, *Charles Dickens* (1985, 7–20); James R. Kincaid, *Annoying the Victorians* (1995, 21–34); Steven Marcus, *Dickens: From Pickwick to Dombey* (1965); J. Hillis Miller, *Charles Dickens: The World of His Novels* (1958, 1–35) and *Topographies* (1995, 105–33). *Pickwick*'s lack of visibility in books driven by historicist modes of inquiry on Dickens is worth noting. Elizabeth Campbell's *Fortune's Wheel: Dickens and the Iconography of Women's Time* (2003) offers no consideration. Anny Sadrin's *Parentage and Inheritance in the Novels of Charles Dickens* (1994) mentions *Pickwick* once only, in a passing reference to the formation of the identity of "Boz." Jeremy Tambling's Foucault-inspired *Dickens, Violence, and the Modern State: Dreams of the Scaffold* (1995) makes only the briefest of references, as I discuss below, in the body of the chapter.

Such is the historicist imperative in criticism of nineteenth-century literature that Bowen's analysis of the early novels, governed as it is by epistemological, linguistic, and other theoretical concerns most effectively deployed through close reading rather than the imposition of a master metaphor or trope that will recuperate texts and erase their differences, is chastised in one review for being "like new criticism" in its "tending to be sealed off from consideration of the 1830s and 1840s" (Tambling 2001, 550). Bizarrely, in a moment that to some will appear marked by an inability to distinguish clearly differing historical moments or to *see* effectively the difference and historicity of such critical moments, Tambling, who seems intent on establishing a family resemblance between Bowen's book and "older Dickens criticism" (549) based chiefly on the partition of Dickens' novels into "earlier" and "later," then accuses Bowen of a construction of Dickens "who has been put together out of modish critical tropes" (549, for which read "Derrida"). Presumably, given Tambling's own work on Dickens, had those critical tropes been "power," "violence," "surveillance," "the state," "the carceral," "the prison" (for which read "Foucault") neither would the reading of Dickens have been a "construction," nor would the tropes have been "modish." Tambling's critique of Bowen's partition of the novels is also somewhat disingenuous, given his own lack of consideration of *Sketches by Boz, Pickwick,* or *Nicholas Nickleby.*

It should not be thought that Tambling's work is deliberately singled out. Lack of space prevents a more extended critique, but one could also include in such remarks D. A. Miller's reading of *Bleak House* in his *The Novel and the Police* (1988, 58–106). Were one to consider assigning ontologies, or imposing critical identities, based on the critical scene, one might wish to suggest, in the wake of work by Miller, Kincaid, Bowen, Marlow, and Connor, that *Pickwick* is Dickens' "poststructuralist" work, and therefore, in its play, its excess, and its difference, resists and exposes the misanthropic paucity of particular historicisms. This last hypothesis would appear to be borne out in Anny Sadrin's passing assessment of Jingle and the two Wellers as the novel's "deconstructors," the justification for this being that in their improvisatory speech there is "no regard for spelling, or grammar, or syntax, or paragraph division or tense sequence" (Sadrin 1993, 27).

4. Rainsford offers a convincing comparison between Dickens' last remarks in his preface to the "Cheap Edition"—"that a few petty boards and bodies . . . are . . . always to keep their little fiddles going, for a Dance of Death"—with the phrases "Loud sport the dancers in the dance of death" and "Timbrels & violins" from Blake's *Milton.*

5. See Marlow (1985, 939) for the comparison of Dickens with Sterne; Jacqueline Simpson offers a sharp comparison between Smollett and Dickens (1983, 463); Juliet McMaster comments on the comparison between Pickwick and Don Quixote (1983, 595). Other articles addressing the Pickwick-Quixote relationship are Steven H. Gale, "Cervantes' Influence on Dickens, with Comparative Emphasis on *Don Quijote* and *Pickwick Papers*" (1973, 135–56); Mercedes Potau, "Notes on Parallels between *The Pickwick Papers* and *Don Quixote*" (1993, 105–110); Angus Easson, "Don Pickwick: Dickens and the Transformation of Cervantes" (2002, 173–88).

6. As is acknowledged in the standard critical studies, introductions, and biographies of Dickens, sales were initially slow. By February 1837, sales had increased to fourteen thousand, and the figure reached its phenomenal peak by the end of that year. Significantly, serialization meant that the novel was much less expensive, at 1s (shilling) per part, than many three-volume novels being published at the same time. Thus, serialization and cost helped the novel reach a wider audience. For a brief discussion of this, see Andrew Sanders, *Charles Dickens* (2003, 19). Also on *Pickwick* and serialization, see Sangwha Moon, "*The Pickwick Papers:* An Encounter of Serial Fiction and Capitalism" (2001, 53–66).

7. On the complexity of the idea of "character" see J. Hillis Miller, "Character," in *Ariadne's Thread: Story Lines* (1992, 28–143).

8. On language, specifically speech and *Logos* as apophansis, see Martin Heidegger, *Being and Time* (1996, 28–29).

9. To take one example, the title page of Richardson's *Clarissa* (1747–48) proclaims that it is "published by the editor of PAMELA."

10. Again, I would like to stress that my primary purpose is not to contextualize Dickens' novel. Nor is it to offer a cultural study of modes of historical perception here. My observation has more to do with what I perceive to be the necessity of reading *Pickwick* differently, and so to attempt to read the difference of *The Pickwick Papers.*

11. Doubtless, it is because of his "failure" to read the significance of signs "correctly" that Dickens appears hardly at all in Gallagher's study. A different "historicist" account of Dickens is to be found in Josephine Guy, *The Victorian Social-Problem Novel* (1996). Daniel Cottom provides a critical account of most of Dickens' novels from a somewhat materialist perspective in his *Ravishing Tradition: Cultural Forces and Literary History* (1996, 112–40). Regardless of the specific details of the historicism or materialism being practiced in each of these studies, what is noticeable is the absence, not only of *Pickwick,* but also the novels of the 1830s, which as well as *Pickwick* are *Oliver Twist* and *Nicholas Nickleby* (*Twist* is mentioned once by Guy). It strikes me as disingenuous in the extreme to claim, as an anonymous reader of this book in early draft form did, that *Pickwick* is not at issue. I would argue that it is at issue precisely because it is visibly noticeable by its absence.

12. In addition to Goodman and Crosby's works already cited, see Adela Pinch, *Strange Fits of Passion: Epistemologies of Emotion, Hume to Austen* (1996), on which Goodman draws in her introduction to *Georgic Modernity.*

Notes to Chapter 2

1. Stephen Kern offers a brief but compelling and insightful analysis of the power of eyes and the gaze, particularly those of Nancy in *Oliver Twist,* in *Eyes of Love: The Gaze in English and French Paintings and Novels, 1840–1900* (1996, 149–52).

2. I have used both words here, as both appear equally to define provisionally what takes place through the appearance of the tales in question. On the one hand, the narratives "seem" to add something unnecessary that alters or disrupts the text; on the other, the interruption causes the presentation of the tale, the "usefulness" or purpose of which in the context of *Pickwick* is, if not immediately clear, then at least to question the very form and structure, if not the constitution and ontology of the novel, and the efficacy of its own narratives. However naïve the question appears, one might be tempted to ask, what does Mr Pickwick's narrative lack that comes to be filled by these, mostly supernatural, cautionary and moral tales? And what, moreover, is the function of these anachronistic narratives in the "modern" world of the early nineteenth century?

3. On the oddity of reading as a form of haunting see J. Hillis Miller, *On Literature* (2002); Nicholas Royle, *The Uncanny* (2003); and Peter Schwenger, *Fantasm and Fiction: On Textual Envisioning* (1999). All three works refer, of course, to Sigmund Freud's essay "The 'Uncanny'" (1913/1985).

4. An indispensable study of visibility in the nineteenth century is Lindsay Smith, *Victorian Photography, Painting and Poetry: The Enigma of Visibility in Ruskin, Morris and the Pre-Raphaelites* (1995).

5. As will be familiar to some, the language of speech act theory derives from the work of J. L. Austin, particularly *How to Do Things with Words* (1975). In broad terms, Austin identifies two principal speech acts, the constative and the performative. A constative speech act would be a description, such as "the sky is blue," where the language of description is seemingly separate from that which it is in the act of representing. A performative speech act, on the other hand, is one that "does" something, such as a promise, wedding vows, or the act of naming ("I name this ship"). For a speech act to be performative, says Austin, it has to be felicitous, that is, true to its context. Therefore, wedding vows in a play or novel are not "true" performatives. However, as Jacques Derrida has demonstrated on a number of occasions, one cannot stabilize a context, and neither can one guarantee the "felicity" of the speech act's utterance. (See Jacques Derrida, *Limited Inc* [1988].) This volume gathers Derrida's earliest essays on speech act theory, including "Signature Event Context," which appears in a different translation in Derrida's *Margins of Philosophy* [1982, 307–30]). Moreover, as Derrida shows, there is always the possibility that a so-called constative speech act can slip into a performative one or, to put this another way, the performative is always already immanent within the constative, as is the case with the sentence and the motion

from one clause to another, concerning Miss Wardle's view of Tracy Tupman. The sentence enacts or performs the very thing it describes. For an extensive, not to say exhaustive consideration of the role of the speech act in literature, see J. Hillis Miller, *Speech Acts in Literature* (2001).

6. Hooke's *Micrographia* was not restricted in its success to scientific societies and the academic community. In his diary of 1665, on 21 January, Samuel Pepys crowds in between the lines of his regular entry, "Before I went to bed, I sat up till 2 a-clock in my chamber, reading of Mr. Hookes Microscopicall Observacions, the most ingenious book that ever I read in my life" (1995, 18). The mid-1660s were an important time for scientific experiment and discovery, particularly with regard to matters relating to light and optics; in the same year as the publication of *Micrographia,* Isaac Newton was laying the grounds for his theory of light and color. As I mention in the body of the chapter, following Barbara Stafford and Kevis Goodman's invaluable research, from the 1660s and throughout the 1700s, in what is termed the long eighteenth century, the question of vision and its related metaphors enter fully into cultural life through scientific, philosophical, and economic discourse.

7. See particularly chapter 8, "Of the Distance of the Picture: The Viewing Subject," 186–222.

8. Elizabeth Deeds Ermath remarks on *Pickwick*'s indebtedness to the picaresque tradition (1997, 36), while in *Charles Dickens: The World of His Novels* (1958) J. Hillis Miller observes of the novel's "Victorian picaresque" that it is "more akin to [Smollett's] *Peregrine Pickle*" and that "it seems to be purely in the manner of the eighteenth-century novel" (22). Miller also comments, however, and rightly so, that *Pickwick,* "so closely linked to eighteenth-century optimism, is really a farewell to the eighteenth century" (34). In his introduction to the Penguin edition of the novel, Mark Wormald outlines some of the literary and cultural antecedents on which Dickens draws, while also acknowledging the "eighteenth-century picaresque fiction Dickens grew up with" (*PP* xiv). For a philosophical contextualization of *Pickwick* in relation to eighteenth-century thought, see William Palmer on the influence of Shaftesbury and Shaftesbury's influence on mid-eighteenth-century novelists, particularly Sterne, on the matter of sentiment (1997, 24–31).

9. Of course, it is impossible to be certain that the "scientific gentleman" is a double of Samuel Pickwick. It is, however, the undecidability that makes this brief, quite literally "unparalleled" appearance uncanny. The effect is all the more discernible, and the reading of doubleness somewhat more insistent due to the anonymity of the "elderly gentleman of scientific attainments." While the anonymous gentleman "delighted all the Scientific Associations beyond measure" (*PP* 532; we cannot help but speculate that the phrase "beyond measure" appears to carry in it an ironic registration of scientific discourse), Mr Pickwick's "Observations on the Theory of Tittlebats" (which, like the scientific gentleman's publication, is designated a "treatise" [*PP* 19]) "agitated the scientific world" (*PP* 16). Also like his doppelganger, Mr Pickwick is described as an "elderly gentleman" (*PP* 400). There are several other "elderly gentlemen" to which the novel refers, and it is not too great an imaginative feat to consider that behind Mr Pickwick's anonymous double, there is projected a world of elderly scientific gentlemen for

whom meaning and identity, source and origin, are always undecidable.

10. While I am not suggesting any direct connection between Dickens and contemporary science, the comic concussion and its illuminating effects offer the reader a brief glimpse into the interests of scientific research in the nineteenth century concerning the physiology of the senses, particularly as that research related to matters of vision and physiological optics. The principal researcher in this field was Johannes Müller (1801–1858), whose understanding of vision and his "notion of the observer [was] radically alien from that of the eighteenth century," as Jonathan Crary argues (1990, 88). (see, especially, chapter 3, "Subjective Vision and the Separation of the Senses" (67–96), from which the citation above and other comments here are taken.) Müller had published "two influential books on vision" (89) both in 1826 and, subsequently, in 1833, his *Handbuch der Physiologie des Menschen,* translated into English in 1842 by Dr William Baly. As Crary shows, Müller discovered that a shock to the optic nerve "produces the experience of light" (90). An entirely coincidental parallel between Dickens and Müller is to be found in the fact that both apprehend "fundamentally arbitrary relation[s] between stimulus and sensation," and hence the capacity, as Crary puts it, and as we have ample evidence in *The Posthumous Papers of the Pickwick Club,* for the observing subject to "*misperceive,*" because the eye "renders differences equivalent" (90). Misperception is all too common in *Pickwick,* as a number of the quotations and the passages from which they come demonstrate.

Notes to Chapter 3

1. On the historical constructedness and production of the male bourgeois subject and, with that, the notion of modernity, see Francis Barker, *The Tremulous Private Body: Essays on Subjection* (1984), and Peter de Bolla, *The Discourse of the Sublime* (1989). More generally, for arguments concerning the modernity of English identity as this is articulated between the late seventeenth century and the early nineteenth century, see Peter Ackroyd, *Notes for a New Culture* (1976, rev. ed. 1993); Linda Colley, *Britons: Forging the Nation, 1707–1837* (1992); John Lucas, *England and Englishness: Ideas of Nationhood in English Poetry, 1688–1900* (1990); and Richard Price, *British Society, 1680–1880: Dynamism, Conformity, and Change* (1999).

2. Translation mine.

3. Implicit in my argument is a ghostly communication between Ackroyd's insistence on cultural inheritance and Derrida's enigmatic figure of the anachronistic contemporary. Were there space, I would like to argue for a reading of Samuel Pickwick as an "anachronistic" contemporary of the readers of *The Pickwick Papers* in the late 1830s, whose anachronistic survival in terms of that spectral Englishness (to which I have alluded) is signalled as an effect of writing and translation in the proper name "Samuel" (on which I comment below in the present chapter).

4. It will be observed frequently that identities and meanings are confused, exceeded, disturbed, and denied throughout *The Pickwick Papers.* Indeed, the novel relies on the eruption of impropriety from within the proper, whether the

event concerns merely the improper use of an object or involves the depiction of a social gathering. An event is transformed into a spectacle, that is to say, there is what I would like to describe as a translation effect that takes place from within a given identity, whereby something emerges from within itself as its own parody, becoming thereby a parodic critique through the emphasis on the visual aspects of *spectacle* of the social and cultural worlds of early nineteenth-century England through the rhetorical emphasis on excess, misunderstanding, and failed communications.

5. See also J. Hillis Miller, "Sam Weller's Valentine: Dickens," in *Topographies* (1995, 105–33).

6. See Joseph Rosenblum, "*The Pickwick Papers* and *Paradise Lost*" (1986).

7. The double million gas microscope was being marketed in 1837 (gas being the source of illumination), as Mark Wormald informs us in a note to the Penguin edition (*PP* 793 n. 11). As we can see from this, Wormald is correct to suggest on several occasions that Dickens has a "bold" way with his source materials. However, it can also be remarked that historical accuracy is not, in effect, an issue for Dickens; more generally, literature, as I remark elsewhere, is irreducible to fact, date, or event, and Dickens should perhaps be read with an eye directed more to the spirit, rather than the letter of the historical.

Notes to Afterword

1. In shaping this argument, I am drawing on two sources, although I do not cite them directly: Jacques Derrida, "'Le Parjure,' *Perhaps:* Storytelling and Lying ('abrupt breaches of syntax')" (2002, 195–234); and J. Hillis Miller, *Reading Narrative* (1998). See particularly "The Anacoluthonic Lie," 149–57.

2. Derrida invokes the necessary relationship between feeling—translatable, however peremptorily, as sentiment—and accountability and responsibility in "The Principle of Reason" (2004a, 155).

3. The stresses on *remain/s* in the sentence should serve to draw the reader's attention to seeing how the temporal dimension is at work within a single word and across its iterable use; a traversal is performed here, which, in its semantic oscillation brings into view, albeit somewhat obliquely, how a sign can both *remain* the same and yet not the same, how past, present, and future are signalled while their absolute, discrete boundaries are erased, or at least crossed, in the motion I have sought to enact graphically.

4. On the temporal fold, the other, and the notion of *invention* that I am invoking here, see Jacques Derrida, "Psyche: Inventions of the Other" (1989, 56).

Works Cited

Ackroyd, Peter. *Notes for a New Culture.* (1976) Rev. edition. London: Alkin Books, 1993.

———. *Dickens.* London: Sinclair-Stevenson, 1990.

Agacinski, Sylviane. *Time Passing: Modernity and Nostalgia.* (2000) Trans. Jody Gladding. New York: Columbia University Press, 2003.

Arac, Jonathan. *Commissioned Spirits: The Shaping of Social Motion in Dickens, Carlyle, Melville, and Hawthorne.* New Brunswick, N.J.: Rutgers University Press, 1979.

Ashton, Rosemary. "Introduction" to George Eliot, *Middlemarch.* (1871–72) London: Penguin, 2003. vii–xxii.

Augé, Marc. *Oblivion.* (1998) Trans. Marjolijn de Jager. Foreword James E. Young. Minneapolis: University of Minnesota Press, 2004.

Austin, J. L. *How to Do Things with Words.* (1962) 2nd edition, ed. J. O. Urmson and Marina Sbisà. Cambridge, Mass.: Harvard University Press, 1975.

Bal, Mieke. *Travelling Concepts in the Humanities: A Rough Guide.* Toronto: University of Toronto Press, 2002.

Barker, Francis. *The Tremulous Private Body: Essays on Subjection.* London: Methuen, 1984.

Benjamin, Walter. "The Signatures of the Age." (1936) In *Selected Writings, Volume 3: 1935–1938.* Trans. Edmund Jephcott and others. Ed. Howard Eiland and Michael W. Jennings. Cambridge, Mass.: The Belknap Press, 2002a. 139–40.

———. "Theory of Distraction." (1936) In *Selected Writings, Volume 3: 1935–1938.* Trans. Edmund Jephcott and others. Ed. Howard Eiland and Michael W. Jennings. Cambridge, Mass.: The Belknap Press, 2002b, 142–43.

———. "On the Concept of History." (1940) In *Selected Writings, Volume 4: 1938–1940.* Trans. Edmund Jephcott and others. Ed. Howard Eiland and Michael W. Jennings. Cambridge, Mass.: The Belknap Press, 2003. 389–400.

Bennington, Geoffrey. "Derridabase." In Geoffrey Bennington and Jacques Derrida, *Jacques Derrida.* (1991) Trans. Geoffrey Bennington. Chicago: University of Chicago Press, 1993. 3–317.

Bergson, Henri. *Matter and Memory.* (1908) Trans. N. M. Paul and W. S. Palmer. New York: Zone Books, 1999.

Bevis, Matthew. "Temporizing Dickens." *Review of English Studies: A Quarterly Journal of English Literature and the English Language* 52:206 (May 2001): 171–91.

Bodenheimer, Rosemarie. "Knowing and Telling in Dickens's Retrospects." In Suzy Anger, ed., *Knowing the Past: Victorian Literature and Culture.* Ithaca, N.Y.: Cornell University Press, 2001. 215–33.

Bowen, John. *Other Dickens: Pickwick to Chuzzlewit.* Oxford: Oxford University Press, 2000.

Brannigan, John. *New Historicism and Cultural Materialism.* Basingstoke: Macmillan, 1998.

Campbell, Elizabeth. *Fortune's Wheel: Dickens and the Iconography of Women's Time.* Athens: Ohio University Press, 2003.

Carlyle, Thomas. *Signs of the Times.* (1829) In *Selected Writings.* Ed. and int. Alan Shelston. London: Penguin, 1986. 61–85.

———. *Sartor Resartus.* (1833–34) Ed. Kerry McSweeney and Peter Sabor. Oxford: Oxford University Press, 1991.

Castle, Terry. *The Female Thermometer: Eighteenth-Century Culture and the Invention of the Uncanny.* New York: Oxford University Press, 1995.

Chittick, Kathryn. "*Pickwick Papers* and the *Sun.*" *Nineteenth-Century Fiction* 39:3 (December 1984): 328–35.

———. *Dickens and the 1830s.* Cambridge: Cambridge University Press, 1990.

Cohen, Tom. *Ideology and Inscription: "Cultural Studies" after Benjamin, de Man, and Bakhtin.* Cambridge: Cambridge University Press, 1998.

Colebrook, Claire. *Ethics and Representation: From Kant to Post-structuralism.* Edinburgh: Edinburgh University Press, 1999.

Colley, Linda. *Britons: Forging the Nation, 1707–1837.* London: Pimlico, 1992.

Connor, Stephen. *Charles Dickens.* Oxford: Basil Blackwell, 1985.

Conrad, Joseph. "Preface." *The Nigger of the "Narcissus."* (1897) Ed. and int. Cedric Watts. London: Penguin, 1988.

Costa Lima, Luiz. *Control of the Imaginary: Reason and Imagination in Modern Times.* (1984) Trans. Ronald W. Sousa. Afterword Jochen Schulte-Sasse. Minneapolis: University of Minnesota Press, 1988.

Cottom, Daniel. *Ravishing Tradition: Cultural Forces and Literary History.* Ithaca, N.Y.: Cornell University Press, 1996.

Crary, Jonathan. "Modernizing Vision." In Hal Foster, ed., *Vision and Visuality,* vol. 2. Seattle: Bay Press, 1988. 29–50.

———. *Techniques of the Observer: On Vision and Modernity in the Nineteenth Century.* Cambridge, Mass.: MIT Press, 1990.

Crosby, Christina. *The Ends of History: Victorians and "the Woman Question."* London: Routledge, 1991.

Dart, Geoffrey. "The Cockney Moment (The Character of the "Cockney" in Dickens's *Pickwick Papers* and *Sketches by Boz*)." *Cambridge Quarterly* 32:3 (2003): 203–23.

de Bolla, Peter. *The Discourse of the Sublime: Readings in History, Aesthetics, and the Subject.* Oxford: Blackwell, 1989.

de Man, Paul. *The Rhetoric of Romanticism.* New York: Columbia University Press, 1984.

———. *The Resistance to Theory.* Minneapolis: University of Minnesota Press, 1986.

———. *Aesthetic Ideology.* Ed. and int. Andrzej Warminski. Minneapolis: University of Minnesota Press, 1996.

Derrida, Jacques. *Margins of Philosophy.* (1972) Trans. Alan Bass. Chicago: University of Chicago Press, 1982.

———. *The Post Card: From Socrates to Freud and Beyond.* (1980) Trans. Alan Bass. Chicago: University of Chicago Press, 1987.

———. *Limited Inc.* Trans. Samuel Weber et al. Evanston, Ill.: Northwestern University Press, 1988.

———. "Psyché: Inventions of the Other." Trans. Catherine Porter. In Lindsay Waters and Wlad Godzich, eds., *Reading de Man Reading.* Minneapolis: University of Minnesota Press, 1989. 25–65.

———. *Archive Fever: A Freudian Impression.* Trans. Eric Prenowitz. Chicago: University of Chicago Press, 1996a.

———. "'As if I were Dead': an Interview with Jacques Derrida." In John Brannigan, Ruth Robbins, and Julian Wolfreys, eds., *Applying: to Derrida.* Basingstoke: Macmillan, 1996b. 211–26.

———. *Of Grammatology.* (1967) Corrected ed., trans. Gayatri Chakravorty Spivak. Baltimore, Md.: The Johns Hopkins University Press, 1998.

———. *The Work of Mourning.* Ed. Pascale-Anne Brault and Michael Naas. Chicago: University of Chicago Press, 2001.

———. "'Le parjure.' Perhaps: Storytelling and Lying ('abrupt breaches of syntax')." Trans. Peggy Kamuf. In Carol Jacobs and Henry Sussman, eds., *Acts of Narrative.* Stanford, Calif.: Stanford University Press, 2003. 195–234.

———. "The Principle of Reason: The University in the Eyes of Its Pupils." (1983) Trans. Catherine Porter and Edward P. Morris. In *Eyes of the University: Right to Philosophy 2.* Trans. Jan Plug et al. Stanford, Calif.: Stanford University Press, 2004a. 129–55.

———. "'Je suis en guerre contre moi-même': entretien avec Jean Birnbaum." *Le Monde* (18572) 12 October 2004b. 6–7.

———. "Composing 'Circumfession.'" In John D. Caputo and Michael J. Scanlon, eds., *Augustine and Postmodernism: Confessions and Circumfession.* Bloomington: Indiana University Press, 2005. 19–27.

Dickens, Charles. *The Life and Adventures of Nicholas Nickleby.* (1838–39) Ed. Michael Slater. London: Penguin, 1986.

———. *The Dent Uniform Edition of Dickens' Journalism. Volume 1: Sketches by Boz and Other Early Papers, 1833–39.* Ed. Michael Slater. London: J. M. Dent, 1994.

———. *The Dent Uniform Edition of Dickens' Journalism. Volume 2: The Amusements of the People and Other Papers: Reports, Essays and Reviews, 1834–1851.* Ed. Michael Slater. London: J. M. Dent, 1996a.

———. *The Personal History of David Copperfield.* (1850) Ed. and int. Jeremy Tambling. London: Penguin, 1996b.

———. *Selected Journalism, 1850–1870.* Ed. David Pascoe. London: Penguin, 1997.

———. *The Posthumous Papers of the Pickwick Club.* (1836–37) Ed. and int. Mark Wormald. London: Penguin, 2003.

Easson, Angus. "Don Pickwick: Dickens and the Transformation of Cervantes." In Alice Jenkins and Juliet Johns, eds., *Rereading Victorian Fiction.* Foreword John Sutherland. Basingstoke: Palgrave Macmillan, 2002. 173–88.

Edgecombe, Rodney Stenning. "Comic Hypotheses in *The Pickwick Papers.*" *Dickens Quarterly* 7:4 (December 1990): 359–70.

Eliot, George. "The Natural History of German Life: Riehl." In Thomas Pinney, ed., *Essays of George Eliot.* London: Routledge and Kegan Paul, 1963. 266–99.

———. "Notes on Form in Art." (1868) In A. S. Byatt and Nicholas Warren, eds., *Selected Essays, Poems and Other Writings.* Int. A. S. Byatt. London: Penguin, 1990. 231–36.

Ermath, Elizabeth Deeds. *The English Novel in History, 1840–1895.* London: Routledge, 1997.

Feltes, N. N. *Modes of Production of Victorian Novels.* Chicago: University of Chicago Press, 1986.

Fenves, Peter. *"Chatter": Language and History in Kierkegaard.* Stanford, Calif.: Stanford University Press, 1993.

Fotí, Véronique. *Vision's Invisibles: Philosophical Explorations.* Albany: State University of New York Press, 2004.

Foucault, Michel. *The Order of Things.* (1966) New York: Vintage, 1973.

Freud, Sigmund. "The 'Uncanny.'" (1919) In *Gesammelte Werke 12.* London: Imago, 1947. 229–48. Trans. James Strachey. Pelican Freud Library 14. Harmondsworth: Penguin, 1985. 339–76.

Frow, John. *Marxism and Literary History.* Cambridge, Mass.: Harvard University Press, 1986.

Gagnier, Regenia. *Subjectivities: A History of Self-Representation in Britain, 1832–1920.* New York: Oxford University Press, 1991.

Gale, Steven H. "Cervantes' Influence on Dickens, with Comparative Emphasis on *Don Quijote* and *Pickwick Papers.*" *Anales Cervantinos* 12 (1973): 135–56.

Gallagher, Catherine. *The Industrial Reformation of English Fiction: Social Discourse and Narrative Form, 1832–1867.* Chicago: University of Chicago Press, 1985.

Goodman, Kevis. *Georgic Modernity and British Romanticism: Poetry and the Mediation of History.* Cambridge: Cambridge University Press, 2004.

Grass, Sean C. "Pickwick, the Past, and the Prison." *Dickens Studies Annual: Essays on Victorian Fiction* 29 (2000): 17–39.

Grossman, Jonathan H. "Representing Pickwick: The Novel and the Law Courts." *Nineteenth-Century Literature* 52:2 (September 1997): 171–97.

Guy, Josephine. *The Victorian Social-Problem Novel: The Market, the Individual, and Communal Life.* Basingstoke: Macmillan, 1996.

Hartley, L. P. *The Go-Between.* (1953) Int. Douglas Brooks-Davis. London: Penguin, 2004.

Hartman, Geoffrey. "Looking Back on Paul de Man." In Lindsay Waters and Wlad Godzich, eds., *Reading de Man Reading.* Minneapolis: University of Minnesota Press, 1989. 3–24.

Heidegger, Martin. *Being and Time.* (1953) Trans. Joan Stambaugh. Albany: State University of New York Press, 1996.

Hooke, Robert. *Micrographia.* (1665). Palo Alto: Octavo Digital Rare Books, 1998.

Horton, Susan R. "Were They Having Fun Yet? Victorian Optical Gadgetry, Modernist Selves." In Carol T. Christ and John O. Jordan, eds., *Victorian Literature and the Victorian Visual Imagination.* Berkeley and Los Angeles: University of California Press, 1995. 1–26.

Huyssen, Andreas. *Present Pasts: Urban Palimpsests and the Politics of Memory.* Stanford, Calif.: Stanford University Press, 2003.

Kamuf, Peggy. *Book of Addresses.* Stanford, Calif.: Stanford University Press, 2005.

Kant, Immanuel. "Dreams of a Visionary Explained by Dreams of Metaphysics." (1766) In Carl J. Friedrich, ed. and trans., *The Philosophy of Kant.* New York: Modern Library, 1993. 15–20.

Kaplan, Fred. *Dickens: A Biography.* New York: William Morrow & Company, 1988.

Kern, Stephen. *Eyes of Love: The Gaze in English and French Paintings and Novels, 1840–1900.* London: Reaktion Books, 1996.

Kincaid, James R. *Annoying the Victorians.* New York: Routledge, 1995.

Krauss, Rosalind. "The Im/Pulse to See." In Hal Foster, ed., *Vision and Visuality.* Seattle: Bay Press, 1988. 76–85.

Landon, Letitia Elizabeth. *On the Ancient and Modern Influence of Poetry.* (1832) In Thomas J. Collins and Vivienne J. Rundle, eds., *The Broadview Anthology of Victorian Poetry and Poetic Theory.* Peterborough, Ont.: Broadview Press, 1999. 1206–11.

Liu, Alan. *Wordsworth: The Sense of History.* Stanford, Calif.: Stanford University Press, 1989.

Lucas, John. *England and Englishness: Ideas of Nationhood in English Poetry, 1688–1900.* London: The Hogarth Press, 1990.

Lukács, Georg. *History and Class Consciousness: Studies in Marxist Dialectics.* Trans. Rodney Livingstone. Cambridge, Mass.: MIT Press, 1972.

Marcus, Stephen. *Dickens: From Pickwick to Dombey.* London: Chatto and Windus, 1965.

———. "Language into Structure: Pickwick Revisited." In Harold Bloom, ed., *Modern Critical Views: Charles Dickens.* New York: Chelsea House, 1987. 183–202.

Marion, Jean-Luc. *The Crossing of the Visible.* (1996) Trans. K. A. Smith. Stanford, Calif.: Stanford University Press, 2004.

Marlow, James E. "Pickwick's Writing: Propriety and Language." *ELH* 52:4 (Winter 1985): 939–63.

Marrati, Paola. *Genesis and Trace: Derrida Reading Husserl and Heidegger.* Trans. Simon Sparks. Stanford, Calif.: Stanford University Press, 2005.

McMaster, Juliet. "Visual Design in *Pickwick Papers.*" *Studies in English Literature 1500–1900* 23:4 (1983): 595–614.

Merleau-Ponty, Maurice. *The Visible and the Invisible.* (1964) Trans. Alphonso Lingis. Ed. Claude Lefort. Evanston: Northwestern University Press, 1968.

Miller, D. A. *The Novel and the Police.* Berkeley: University of California Press, 1988.

Miller, J. Hillis. *Charles Dickens: The World of His Novels.* Cambridge, Mass.: Harvard University Press, 1958.

———. *The Ethics of Reading: Kant, de Man, Eliot, Trollope, James, and Benjamin.* New York: Columbia University Press, 1987.

———. *Theory Now and Then.* Hemel Hempstead: Harvester Wheatsheaf, 1991.

———. *Ariadne's Thread: Story Lines.* New Haven, Conn.: Yale University Press, 1992.

———. *Topographies.* Stanford, Calif.: Stanford University Press, 1995.

———. *Reading Narrative.* Norman: University of Oklahoma Press, 1998.

———. *Speech Acts in Literature.* Stanford, Calif.: Stanford University Press, 2001.

———. *On Literature.* London: Routledge, 2002.

———. "The Degree Zero of Criticism." In Julian Wolfreys, *Thinking Difference: Critics in Conversation.* New York: Fordham University Press, 2004a. 147–64.

———. "Why Literature? A Profession: An Interview with J. Hillis Miller." In Julian Wolfreys, ed., *The J. Hillis Miller Reader.* Edinburgh: Edinburgh University Press, 2004b. 405–422.

Moon, Sangwha. "*The Pickwick Papers:* An Encounter of Serial Fiction and Capitalism." *Nineteenth-Century Literature in English* 5 (2001): 53–66.

Musselwhite, David E. *Partings Welded Together: Politics and Desire in the Nineteenth-Century English Novel.* London: Methuen, 1987.

Palmer, William J. *Dickens and the New Historicism.* New York: St. Martin's Press, 1997.

Patten, Robert L. "*Pickwick Papers* and the Development of Serial Fiction." *Rice University Studies* 61:1 (1975): 51–74.

Pepys, Samuel. *The Diary of Samuel Pepys, Volume VI, 1665.* Ed. R. C. Latham and W. Matthews. London: Harper Collins, 1995.

Pinch, Adela. *Strange Fits of Passion: Epistemologies of Emotion, Hume to Austen.* Stanford, Calif.: Stanford University Press, 1996.

Potau, Mercedes. "Notes on Parallels between *The Pickwick Papers* and *Don Quixote.*" *Dickens Quarterly* 10:2 (June 1993): 105–10.

Price, Richard. *British Society, 1680–1880: Dynamism, Conformity, and Change.* Cambridge: Cambridge University Press, 1999.

Rainsford, Dominic. *Authorship, Ethics and the Reader: Blake, Dickens, Joyce.* Basingstoke: Macmillan, 1997.

Ricciardi, Alessia. *The Ends of Mourning: Psychoanalysis, Literature, Film.* Stanford, Calif.: Stanford University Press, 2003.

Ricoeur, Paul. *Memory, History, Forgetting.* Trans. Kathleen Blamey and David Pellauer. Chicago: University of Chicago Press, 2004.

Rigney, Ann. *Imperfect Histories: The Elusive Past and the Legacy of Romantic Historicism.* Ithaca, N.Y.: Cornell University Press, 2001.

Rosenblum, Joseph. "*The Pickwick Papers* and *Paradise Lost.*" *Dickens Quarterly* 3 (1986): 47–54.

Royle, Nicholas. *The Uncanny.* London: Routledge, 2003.

Rubin, Stan S. "Spectator and Spectacle: Narrative Evasion and Narrative Voice in *The Pickwick Papers*." *Journal of Narrative Technique* 6 (1976): 188–203.

Sadrin, Anny. "Fragmentation in *The Pickwick Papers*." *Dickens Studies Annual: Essays on Victorian Fiction* 22 (1993): 21–34.

———. *Parentage and Inheritance in the Novels of Charles Dickens.* Cambridge: Cambridge University Press, 1994.

Sage, Victor. *Le Fanu's Gothic: The Rhetoric of Darkness.* London: Palgrave Macmillan, 2004.

Said, Edward. *Beginnings: Intention and Method.* New York: Basic Books, 1975.

Sanders, Andrew. *Charles Dickens.* Oxford: Oxford University Press, 2003.

Schlicke, Paul, ed. *Oxford Reader's Companion to Dickens.* Oxford: Oxford University Press, 1999.

Schwenger, Peter. *Fantasm and Fiction: On Textual Envisioning.* Stanford, Calif.: Stanford University Press, 1999.

Scott, Charles E. *The Time of Memory.* Albany: State University of New York Press, 1999.

Siegert, Bernhard. *Relays: Literature as an Epoch of the Postal System.* (1993) Trans. Kevin Repp. Stanford, Calif.: Stanford University Press, 1999.

Simpson, Jacqueline. "Urban Legends in *The Pickwick Papers*." *Journal of American Folklore* 96:382 (1983): 462–70.

Smith, Grahame. *The Novel and Society: Defoe to George Eliot.* London: Batsford, 1984.

Smith, Lindsay. *Victorian Photography, Painting and Poetry: The Enigma of Visibility in Ruskin, Morris and the Pre-Raphaelites.* Cambridge: Cambridge University Press, 1995.

Stabler, Jane. *Burke to Byron, Barbauld to Baillie, 1790–1830.* Basingstoke: Palgrave Macmillan, 2002.

Stafford, Barbara Maria. *Artful Science: Enlightenment Entertainment and the Eclipse of Visual Education.* Cambridge, Mass.: MIT Press, 1994.

Steedman, Carolyn. *Dust: The Archive and Cultural History.* New Brunswick, N.J.: Rutgers University Press, 2002.

Stone, Harry. *The Night Side of Dickens: Cannibalism, Passion, Necessity.* Columbus: The Ohio State University Press, 1994.

Tambling, Jeremy. *Dickens, Violence, and the Modern State: Dreams of the Scaffold.* Basingstoke: Macmillan, 1995.

———. "Introduction" to Charles Dickens, *David Copperfield.* London: Penguin, 1996. vii–xxii.

———. Review of John Bowen, *Other Dickens: Pickwick to Chuzzlewit,* and Andrew Sanders, *Dickens and the Spirit of the Age. Nineteenth-Century Literature* 55:4 (March 2001): 548–552.

Trotter, David. "Dickens's Idle Men." In John Schad, ed., *Dickens Refigured: Bodies, Desires, and Other Histories.* Manchester: Manchester University Press, 1996.

Vasseleu, Cathryn. *Textures of Light: Vision and Touch in Irigaray, Levinas, and Merleau-Ponty.* London: Routledge, 1998.

Welsh, Alexander. "Waverly, Pickwick, and Don Quixote." *Nineteenth-Century Fiction* 22 (1967–68): 19–20.

Williams, Raymond. *Marxism and Literature.* Oxford: Oxford University Press, 1977.

———. *Politics and Letters: Interviews with the New Left Review.* London: Verso, 1981.

———. *Writing in Society.* London: Verso, 1983.

Wolfreys, Julian. *Writing London: The Trace of the Urban Text from Blake to Dickens.* Basingstoke: Macmillan, 1998.

———. *Writing London, Vol. 2: Materiality, Memory, Spectrality.* Basingstoke: Palgrave Macmillan, 2004.

Index

Victorian Critical Interventions
Donald E. Hall, Series Editor

This series showcases provocative contributions to Victorian cultural studies that make brash and revisionary claims. Pertinent manuscripts examine any of a wide variety of "texts": literary, religious, political/historical, art- or music-related, gender/sexuality-related, science- or class-related, or even that of Victorian studies itself.

Detecting the Nation: Fictions of Detection and the Imperial Venture
Caroline Reitz

Novel Professions: Interested Disinterest and the Making of the Professional in the Victorian Novel
Jennifer Ruth